PRAISE

"Where was this book when I was a children's ministry pastor? I never felt like I had enough passionate, talented volunteers and it hurt my heart every time one of them left me. Darren Kizer, Christine Kreisher and Steph Whitacre get right to the heart of the matter in *The Volunteer Project*. Full of sound strategy to stop the begging and move to engaging and retaining your most valuable asset, this book is a must read for every ministry leader."

Sherry Surratt
Former CEO and President of MOPS International,
Author and Ministry Veteran

"I've had the honor of traveling around the country with Darren, going from church to church to see how he works with and leads volunteers. Get ready to change the way you look at the world of volunteerism!"

Jon Acuff
New York Times Bestselling Author and Speaker

"*The Volunteer Project* sizzles with energy and ideas! As I started reading, I instantly found that it was full of strategies that I wanted to apply in my ministry. Personally, I have seen Christine put in to practice the principles she shares by helping coach GT Church volunteers to excellence by finding their sweet spot. The Volunteer Project is more than just a book; it is an opportunity to be mentored by three amazing leaders! For anyone working with volunteers, this book is water in the desert and will be one that you will treasure as you develop a zero recruitment culture."

Tom Rees
Director of Church Planting and Development, PennDel Ministries Network

The Volunteer Project
Stop Recruiting. Start Retaining.

Darren Kizer
Christine Kreisher
Steph Whitacre

The Volunteer Project: Stop Recruiting. Start Retaining
Published by Orange, a division of The reThink Group, Inc.
5870 Charlotte Lane, Suite 300
Cumming, GA 30040 U.S.A.

The Orange logo is a registered trademark of The reThink Group, Inc.

All rights reserved. No portion of this book may be reproduced, stored in a retrieval system, or transmitted in any form or by any means—electronic, mechanical, photocopy, recording, scanning, or other—except for brief quotations in critical reviews or articles, without the prior written permission of the publisher.

The website addresses recommended throughout this book are offered as a resource to you. These websites are not intended in any way to be or imply an endorsement on the part of The ReThink Group, nor do we vouch for their content.

Unless otherwise noted, all Scripture quotations are taken from the Holy Bible, New International Version® (NIV®), copyright 1973, 1978, 1984, 2011 by International Bible Society. Used by permission of Zondervan.

Other Orange products are available online and direct from the publisher. Visit our website at www.ThinkOrange.com for more resources like these.

ISBN: 978-1-63570-087-9

Copyright © 2015, 2018 D. Kizer, C. Kreisher, S. Whitacre
Cover Design: Staci Focht

Printed in the United States of America
First Edition 2018

1 2 3 4 5 6 7 8 9 10

03/26/2019

DEDICATION

If you've ever changed the diaper of a baby you just met or sat through the elementary school concert of a kid who does not share your last name, we wrote this for you. If you've taken vacation time to sleep on a gym floor surrounded by stinky middle school students or spent a Friday evening with your arm around a crying high schooler, your heart is at the core of this book. If you know how to rock a fluorescent safety vest like you're walking the runway, it's your charisma that inspires us. If you wake before sunrise to arrive at your post or practice for hours to be prepared to do a job for which you will never receive a paycheck, we dedicate this book to you.

It's you who keep our churches and organizations moving forward. Thank you, Volunteers.

CONTENTS

Acknowledgments — i

Introduction — 1

STRATEGY 1: CELEBRATE THEIR SIGNIFICANCE

1. Their Place In the Vision — 11
2. Find the Sweet Spot — 19
3. Show the Numbers — 25
4. Continual Improvement — 31
5. Showing Appreciation — 35

STRATEGY 2: PROVIDE FIRST-CLASS SUPPORT

6. Train for Success — 43
7. Communicate Early and Often — 53
8. Weekly Huddles — 59
9. Make It Safe — 65
10. Organizing Volunteer Teams — 75

STRATEGY 3: FUEL MEANINGFUL CONNECTIONS

11	Friendship-Friendly Programming	87
12	Make It Fun!	93
13	Planning Connections	97
14	Get It On The Calendar	103
15	Community Can Be Messy	107

STRATEGY 4: EMPOWER THEIR PASSIONS

16	Inviting with Intentionality	115
17	Set Them Free	123
18	Cut The Red Tape	129
19	Make It Helpful	133
20	Volunteers Who Multiply	139

Imagine If . . .	143
Looking for More?	145
Resources and References	147

ACKNOWLEDGMENTS

This project was completed with the support of family and friends who cheered us on. Thank you for meeting us for coffee, being sounding boards for ideas, and celebrating even the smallest milestones. *Darren* would like to thank Becky, Brynn, and Tucker for decades of inspiration, adventure, and mischief. *Christine* would like to thank her best friend, and husband, Jim for pushing her to fulfill her dreams even when it's meant putting his own on hold. She would also like to thank her sons Jason, Jordan, and Jimmy whose encouraging words of "Mom, we're proud of who you are and what you do!" have inspired her to keep writing. ILY! And this page would be incomplete without thanking Deb Bube, who 17 years ago, took Christine under her wing and changed her life by modeling the four strategies found in this book. *Steph* would like to thank Tim for the physical and mental space to create and for not minding when she covers the dining room table with index cards. She would also like to thank her parents for being her earliest and strongest memory of what it looks like to serve others.

Thank you to Dr. David Kizer for his help in the editing process, and for always encouraging me (Darren) to pursue my dreams and take risks. Thank you as well to Karen Troutman—there aren't enough oat bran pancakes in the world to balance the wisdom you dispensed in this project. Thank you to Kellie Graeff and Jeanette Keylor for their help with proofing, and to Becky Kizer for her insight and beautiful laughter every step of the way. Thank you to Staci Focht for her work on the cover design and for making us look good.

Our adventures have taken us all over the world. We spent hours wandering around the Dubai Mall and the town of Jim Thorpe, talking about best practices and sampling the world's best honeys and gelato. The Bagel Bunch, Silver Spoon Diner, Arrowhead Lake, Delta Sky Club, and Roger's wit fueled us to move forward.

Darren would like to thank Trenton Cohort 1 and Dr. Judith Merz of Nova Southeastern University, for their guidance in his doctoral dissertation on volunteer satisfaction. The results of that research are being used to improve volunteer cultures in piles of local churches and nonprofits.

Thank you to Charthouse Learning for your FISH! Philosophy based on the Pike Place Fish Market, which inspired much of our thinking on creating irresistible team environments . . . and gave us permission to shout and throw fish at each other.

Orange brought us together, and life would not be the same without the friendships and learning we have discovered and cultivated within their community of churches and leaders.

The volunteers we have had the privilege of calling friends have made our lives fuller. Thank you to Cheryl Cox and the volunteers of Gateway Church in Dubai, for inviting us to spend time among you in September 2013. It was in your community theatre, homes, and Friday morning gathering where this book was given its heart. Darren and Steph are honored to have spent time dreaming big, rethinking normal, and loving on families alongside the volunteers and staff of Parker Hill Community Church. Likewise, Christine's heart is full of gratitude for the amazing volunteers of GT Church in Reading, Pennsylvania, and for GT's staff who value volunteers for *who* they are and not *what* they do.

INTRODUCTION

Our Zero Recruitment Dream

Have you ever had more volunteers than you needed? You didn't have to ask for help; they just poured in your doors. We've experienced these seasons of ministry, and we loved them! Our experiences and research have brought us to believe unashamedly that it's possible to experience volunteer cultures where zero recruitment is necessary.

In fact, this book is inspired by our dream to see zero recruitment cultures spring up in churches and organizations everywhere. Our desire is that by implementing the strategies found in the following pages, those who lead volunteers will discover the success that comes when you stop trying to recruit new volunteers and instead start focusing on retaining current volunteers.

It's baffling to consider how one volunteer culture can excel beyond others with similar facilities, budgets, and leadership teams. Especially during periods of low volunteer participation, leaders may pause to ask why other ministries are excelling in volunteer participation, while their own struggles. We have studied volunteer data within numerous churches and nonprofit organizations, and have concluded the difference lies within the volunteer culture. Zero recruitment leaders have crafted a culture that is irresistible and attractive.

Zero recruitment cultures . . .
    always have enough volunteers.
    design atmospheres that feel electric.
    draw the best leaders.
    are wildly productive while simultaneously full of laughter.

Volunteers in zero recruitment cultures describe their roles as . . .
    life giving.
    full of opportunity to make new friends.
    fueling their pursuit of meaning.
    enjoyable.
    propelling them forward at home and work.

Our goal is to help you experience a volunteer culture in which you can stop recruiting and start retaining. Don't get us wrong—we're not saying you'll never need to recruit volunteers again. If you're in a growing ministry (which we hope you are), the launching of a new program or site will place you in recruitment mode. When we say to **stop recruiting** and **start retaining**, here's what we mean: *If you choose to stop recruiting and start retaining, you can focus on retention and make that your passion. And if you value your volunteers above your programs, you will create a culture that makes retention easier and attracts additional volunteers.*

The problem is that far too often the immediacy of empty volunteer positions lures us into pouring the majority of our energy into recruitment. When you focus primarily on recruitment, you will continually focus on orienting and engaging a stream of new volunteers. The more time you spend recruiting, the less time you spend investing in current volunteers. Keep in mind that

STOP RECRUITING. START RETAINING.

volunteers are not a renewable resource. That's why it's paramount to celebrate and care for the ones who are already engaged.

Retention should always trump recruitment. It takes exponentially more energy to recruit a volunteer than to retain one. If you adopt a leadership model focused on retention, you will begin to experience a culture where volunteers stick around, and even do much of the recruiting for you by inviting others to join them. Instead of being stuck in an endless cycle of recruit and replace, you'll begin to see your volunteer culture shift to one of enthusiasm and magnetic opportunities.

The Competition

Let's face it, the dynamics of volunteerism have changed significantly in the past decade. More and more nonprofits pop up every day, creating competition for the valuable time of potential volunteers. So with an increasing number of nonprofits to choose from, which organizations win the game? We believe the churches and organizations that win the competition for volunteers are the ones that are intentional about assessing, evaluating, and continually improving their volunteer culture.

A friend of mine (Christine) recently approached me and asked for help in finding a volunteer opportunity. I was confused because I thought he already had a volunteer role at an organization desperate for volunteers. He did, but after a few weeks of going and not feeling needed, he felt like maybe it was a waste of time. He said he was looking for an opportunity where he would be provided direction and support, have a chance to make new friends, and be able to put his gifts to use.

We all know of stories like this one. Volunteers move on to new organizations every day, often with no explanation to leadership as to why. Some people even give leadership a nice, sugarcoated excuse because they are uncomfortable with tension and conflict. But in order to create a zero recruitment culture, honest feedback and a willingness to improve are critical. What former volunteers *don't* tell leadership, they probably *do* tell their friends. As a matter of fact, I would imagine the statistics aren't that different from the results of research done in the business world. Have you heard of the *Customer Complaint Iceberg* or the *Pyramid of Dissatisfaction*? In it, Adrian Swinscoe draws on a 1999 study conducted by TARP which discovered that for every twenty-six unsatisfied customers, only one will register a formal complaint. Swinscoe goes on to explain how on average, one unhappy customer will tell ten people about their negative experience. Those ten people will on average tell five people the story. That means that potentially fifty people will hear about one bad experience.

Don't let those statistics discourage you though. As you begin to understand volunteers better, you'll unlock your future growth potential. Organizations that understand what makes their volunteers tick are the ones that have been intentional about putting strategies in place to produce a zero recruitment culture. We believe the four strategies found in this book will be extremely valuable in identifying your current reality, as well as helping you prioritize where to focus your energy and resources in the days ahead.

Where We're Coming From

If you're holding this book, chances are that you're passionate about leading volunteers. Volunteerism has played a big part in each of our stories, and we bet that's true of you too. Do you remember your first volunteer role? More than likely, that role was foundational in shaping the course of your life, either by directing a career choice or in shaping your character.

Darren jokes that he volunteered his way into all his paying jobs. Over the last twenty-plus years, he was invited into experiences that were so amazing that he voluntarily gave his time and energy because of what he received. On a few occasions, those rewards were so powerful that they initiated career moves and relocation. He's grateful for the organizations that have invited him into their lives and missions. Most of his deep friendships can be linked to being a volunteer or leading volunteers.

Christine's passion for volunteerism comes from the profound impact volunteering has had on her own life. Twenty years ago, she was far from God and spun by a lifetime of dysfunction, abandonment, and pain. She is blown away by how God has used her life, and it all started when someone tapped her on the shoulder, pointed out a gift she saw in Christine, and asked her to use it through a volunteer role.

Now Christine is in a full-time ministry role, coaching and equipping volunteers and church leaders. She is so thankful that, despite her past, someone believed in her and saw something in her that she didn't see in herself. She is incredibly grateful that someone asked her to volunteer, and led her on an adventure that changed the trajectory of her life. She believes that what started with volunteering has made her a better wife, mother, friend, and follower of Jesus, and she's passionate about giving others the same opportunity.

Steph began volunteering, at the prompting of a wise mentor, when she was in high school. Outside of her family, the majority of people who shaped her life as a high school and college student did so through volunteer roles. After college, she used Darren's trick against him and volunteered for him until he hired her. Many of Steph's close friendships are with people she led student small groups with, both as staff and a fellow leader. When she moved to a new city in 2014, one of the first things she did was find volunteer roles in which to connect.

The 4 Before and Bottom Lines

In this book, we're going to introduce you to our Zero Recruitment Model of volunteerism. We believe there are strategies every leader can employ to increase the level of volunteer retention within his or her organization. We wholeheartedly believe in these strategies! But we also believe that there are four mindsets that must be true before volunteerism success can take root. In other words, if you miss or fail at any of these four foundational mindsets, you'll be undermining all other pursuits, including the recruitment and retention of volunteers.

Here's what we call *The 4 Before*—the four mindsets every leader should have:

Excellence. No one wants to be part of a mediocre or shoddy system. We define excellence as doing the best with what you have. You may not have marble floors, but you can vacuum. You may not have stage trussing with moving lights, but you can replace a burned out light bulb. You may not have a website with the newest code and flashy graphics, but you can provide up-to-date posts and accurate information. When you have the mindset of excellence, you communicate that you care. Modeling a caring spirit toward facilities, guests, and details foreshadows the care you will give to your most valuable resource: volunteers.

Mission. It is absolutely essential that the mission of your organization be meaningful and easy to understand. It should be compelling in a way that draws people away from all other options because they want to partner with you. Successful leaders have a clear mission and are able to communicate that mission far and wide to others.

Appreciation. Successful leaders are marked by gratitude and an appreciation for others. As a leader in a church or nonprofit, your attitude should be one of gratitude toward those who donate their time. When it comes down to it, people can sense if an organization is marked by obligation and expectation, or if it is dripping with a sense of appreciation. If you want to retain volunteers, you must foster a spirit of esteem for them as individuals and in their roles as volunteers.

Invitation. Unlike country music would have us believe, people do not enjoy going to places where they're not invited. The majority of us avoid unknown territory unless escorted by a guide or friend. An important part of establishing a strong volunteer culture is the presence of a vibrant and welcoming invitation to join. A welcoming culture is marked by invitations coming from several sources, and not just one person. Irresistible invitations are marked by opportunity, not desperation, and are unapologetic in nature. Don't sell the experience short or sabotage it. Many times the things we fail to find enjoyment in are the very things that others are eager to join.

In addition to The 4 Before, there are a few bottom lines you will find woven into *The Volunteer Project*. These ideas are not specific to a single strategy. They're kind of simple and don't need a lot of explanation, but we will reference them periodically. These tweetable threads are an important part of volunteer leadership.

- If you have an excellence problem, you will have a volunteer problem.
- Make it fun! Volunteers don't need another job.
- Volunteers feel appreciated when you value their time, energy, and talents.
- Happy volunteers invite their friends.
- Volunteers are more than the roles they fill. Equip them for life.
- A fulfilled, supported, appreciated, and empowered volunteer is a long-term volunteer.

Let's Do This

When you think about your top three volunteer experiences, what made them great? What about your worst experience? What made it so miserable? When we are speaking or consulting, we will ask volunteers and leaders to tell us about their best and worst volunteer experiences, and we tend to get very similar answers. There are consistent themes that show up every time.

When describing their worst volunteer experiences, people tend to use words and phrases like . . .
  unorganized.
  no clear direction.
  I didn't have friends there.
  too much red tape.
  I felt obligated to stay.

When describing their best volunteer experiences, people tend to say things like . . .
  I had friends there.
  I felt like I belonged.
  I was making a difference.
  I felt supported, valued, and appreciated.

In this book, we'll unpack four proven strategies to attract and keep volunteers that support the positive statements associated with great volunteer experiences. As you read the four strategies, view your organization-wide culture through the lens of smaller clusters. By looking at a single programming timeslot or volunteer team, you will have a greater ability to evaluate and treat the symptoms. You will also begin to identify wins and see success quickly, which can then be applied to the wider culture. Incremental improvement is key in moving closer to a zero recruitment culture.

Are you ready? It's time to **stop recruiting** and **start retaining.**

STRATEGY 1:
CELEBRATE THEIR SIGNIFICANCE

Celebrating the significance of volunteers' investments centers on the leader making a commitment to providing opportunities for volunteers to serve in roles that are a good fit for their skills and interests. It begins with the leader making a mindset shift from just filling volunteer vacancies to connecting volunteers with roles in which they will thrive. Volunteers experiencing significance say things like, "I love making a difference!"

1 THEIR PLACE IN THE VISION

Create fun and meaningful experiences in which volunteers feel what they do is crucial to fulfilling the mission of the organization.

Changing the World

I (Christine) remember being in my late teens, about to graduate from high school, and surrounded by people asking me the typical, daunting question: "What are you going to do with the rest of your life?" Like most eighteen-year-olds, I had no idea what a big question that was, but as a naïve teenager, I did know this: **I was going to change the world.**

In my short eighteen years, I had felt pain, heartache, and loss. My experiences of abandonment and fear left me longing to feel significant. I had grown up watching the loneliness of crime and addiction, and bought into the lie that significance, and ultimately fulfillment, are found in success. In my mind, success was found in financial gain and material possessions. So for ten years, I worked hard at starting and growing several successful businesses. But the more my businesses grew, the less I felt truly successful.

Then along came two of my favorite words: **But God.** With these two words, He can take everything we think we know about life and turn it upside down. I thought success was financial security, **but God** was calling me to look out for others as well. I was living as though significance was all about me, **but God** was calling me into a bigger story interwoven with others.

Shortcake and Significance

People love knowing they're part of a bigger story. That's why it's crucial for leaders to create fun and meaningful experiences in which volunteers feel what they do truly matters. When individuals experience feelings of significance and see the role they play in your organization's mission, you will hear them say things like, *"I am making a difference!"*

Consider a volunteer who helps in her church's nursery. While she may enjoy the role of taking care of infants, her role becomes even more fulfilling when she hears how providing childcare gave parents an opportunity to be in the adult worship gathering. In the adult worship gathering, the father of one of the babies she cared for heard life-changing truth that will alter the future course of his family. Being a part of this bigger story takes a menial task, like changing diapers, and makes it significant.

People who volunteer in a local church or nonprofit organization do not do so because they desire another job. Most individuals' lives are full of vocational and family stressors, to-do lists and errands, home projects and work deadlines. When it comes to volunteering, the average adult is not looking for random ways to spend their time. Instead they are searching for purpose and meaning. They are on a journey to connect their gifts and interests to something bigger than themselves. This search for meaning provides an opportunity for leaders to build a bridge between personal giftedness and eternal value.

STRATEGY 1: CELEBRATE THEIR SIGNIFICANCE

Researchers refer to the use of ones own skills and abilities to make a difference as *participation efficacy*. Volunteers have a belief that participation in your program will bring about a meaningful result. It is important that as leaders we understand that nearly every volunteer arrives with an unstated psychological contract expecting their participation to result in a positive and meaningful outcome for others. Within a faith community, this phenomenon is heightened with volunteers believing they are gifted to accomplish something of eternal value.

This was certainly the case in my first serving experience! My young boys had been attending our church's kids ministry and loving it. I was appreciative of how the church was pouring into my family and knew I should get involved, but felt under qualified and had no idea where to begin. Then one day my friend Carolyn called and said, "Christine, you are great with kids and you are a great cook! The church is looking for a volunteer to cook with kids on Wednesday nights. Do you think you could give it a try?"

When I began teaching cooking to kids, the first few weeks were more like herding cattle than accomplishing anything of eternal value. The kids would come in, we would make a snack, and I would send them home. It did not take long before God began to press on me the opportunity cooking class was for mentoring and imparting spiritual truth. As a volunteer, I became passionate about not wanting to waste the time God had given me with His precious kids.

One night, I rounded up my group of crazy, energetic fourth and fifth grade boys to make strawberry shortcake. As we mixed together the red strawberries with the white cake, we talked about how Jesus' blood covers our sins (or in this case chocolate shavings) and makes us as pure as snow. At the end of the evening, I invited the group of twenty boys to pray the prayer of salvation with me. Many of them did and I was blown away by how God had used me and strawberry shortcake to change these young lives! I cried the entire way home. I had never before experienced anything like that feeling. **I was making a difference!**

A short time later, on New Year's Day, I received a phone call that changed my life. It was my ministry leader, calling to share with me that two of the boys I shared the kitchen with every week had been killed tragically. As I stood in the front of the church during the funeral, sobbing in front of the caskets, I felt an arm slip around me. It was Jared and Dustin's grandmother. Through a choking voice of sadness, she said sixteen words I will never forget, "Christine, I want to thank you because my grandbabies are in heaven now because of you."

In heaven . . . because of me? Because a leader saw my potential and said, "You can make a difference," I got to introduce these boys to a God who loves them. As the words of Jared and Dustin's grandmother sank into my heart, I committed my life to the call of God. The significance I experienced through volunteering was powerful and I stepped up to learn and lead as much as possible because I wanted my life to count.

The task was cooking with kids. The mission was introducing the next generation to a God who knows them intimately and loves them deeply. When Carolyn asked me to teach kids how to find their way around a kitchen, it was a specific enough ask that catered so highly to my interests, it was easy to say yes. What happened when I saw my role within the big picture of kids ministry is what gave me significance and hooked me for the long haul.

As leaders, when we understand the power of pairing personal participation with widespread impact, we approach every volunteer position as a platform to assist each unique individual in discovering their potential. As leaders of volunteers, it is our responsibility to assist them in unlocking and developing hidden or underused gifts. When we approach our volunteers with this mindset, our focus shifts from what *they can do for us* to what *God can*

STRATEGY 1: CELEBRATE THEIR SIGNIFICANCE

do through them. In this manner we are celebrating their significance by doing the hard work of connecting them to opportunities that fulfill their search for meaning.

Unwrapping the Gift

Within most of our ministries and organizations, we have a clear outline of the positions we need filled. I can imagine right now you might be asking the question, *"Is it possible to fill volunteer vacancies, provide meaning to each individual volunteer, and still fulfill the mission of my organization!?"* The good news is yes! When you understand the types of personalities and giftedness that best fills each unique volunteer role, you are better able to communicate with volunteers. And when they are provided with straightforward communication and an understandable job description, volunteers are able to thrive in accomplishing the mission.

A new volunteer is like an unopened present with layers to be unwrapped. As leaders, we get to peel back these layers by providing opportunities for volunteers to use their gifts to make a meaningful difference. God provides each one of us with unique gifts so together we can advance His kingdom. Paul talks about this in Romans 12:4–8:

> For just as each of us has one body with many members, and these members do not all have the same function, so in Christ we, though many, form one body, and each member belongs to all the others. We have different gifts, according to the grace given to each of us. If your gift is prophesying, then prophesy in accordance with your faith; if it is serving, then serve; if it is teaching, then teach; if it is to encourage, then give encouragement; if it is giving, then give generously; if it is to lead, do it diligently; if it is to show mercy, do it cheerfully.

It's a win-win! We have the honor and responsibility of helping individuals discover their unique gifts in serving Christ, and they help fulfill the vision and mission of our organization. That partnership is exactly how God intended it to be.

When you skillfully cast vision, you are connecting a volunteer's inner search for meaning to tangible actions and relationships. Volunteers who feel the exhilaration of thriving in a role become committed to their role within the organization. Once they experience how what they do meets a deep need within them to fulfill God's unique purpose in and through their life, you may find it difficult to convince them to volunteer anywhere else.

I (Steph) love telling the story of when my husband and I first met Darren. Tim and I had been attending the church where Darren was the family ministries pastor, and we had decided it was time for us to jump in and serve. Our previous experience had been with high school students and we believed that age group to be our sweet spot. We set up a meeting to talk with Darren about the possibility of volunteering with high school students and after a few minutes of chit chat, he leaned forward and said, "Here's the deal, I have piles of great high school leaders. I'm wondering if you will consider this: there's a group of fifth graders whose leaders just transitioned out and they need someone to invest in them. I know they are fifth graders now, but we graduate leaders with students, and someday those fifth graders will be in high school."

The other day, one of those former fifth graders asked me if we could meet for coffee. As she plopped down across from me and tossed her car keys on the table, the past seven years burst through my memory and I saw her as a quirky ten-year-old. But she isn't a little girl anymore and she wanted to talk about ideas she has for college and how she hopes God will use her future. Walking out of Starbucks that afternoon, I was thankful that a leader stepped into my life and cast vision for long-term mentoring relationships.

STRATEGY 1: CELEBRATE THEIR SIGNIFICANCE

Without vision and a clearly defined role, I would have missed out on being part of a bigger story.

Deep within each of us is an inner desire to live a life of significance and meaning. We all long for a better future. We want to make a difference. We want to leave the world a better place. Something magical happens when a person's search for significance collides with an opportunity to be a part of something bigger than oneself. He begins a journey of becoming who God created him to be. I don't know about you, but for me there are few greater joys than watching someone's role in God's story unfold.

Next Steps

1. Identify three volunteers who you see making an impact and tell them this week how they are making a difference.

2. Ask five of your volunteers what the vision is of your organization. Use their answers as a standard for how you are doing communicating your vision.

2 FIND THE SWEET SPOT

Assess the sweet spots of volunteers and look for roles in which to help individuals grow.

Identifying Sweet Spots

Everyone can volunteer somewhere, but no one can serve anywhere. Helping potential volunteers find a role that is a fit for their skill sets, personalities, and passions should be a top priority of those who lead volunteers. We refer to helping an individual discover a role that meets this criteria as *finding the sweet spot.*

When a person serves in their sweet spot, the experience is inherently different than serving in any ole' spot. Serving in any ole' spot is characterized by duty, responsibility, and commitment, which can be emotionally draining. On the flip side, time spent serving in *the sweet spot* can be described as life giving, empowering, enjoyable, and invigorating!

If you want to achieve an excellent volunteer culture, your mindset should be *"Are my volunteers in their sweet spots?"* instead of, *"Do I have all the spots filled?"* It can be incredibly hard to make this shift, but if you commit to this principle and lead with excellence, the tide will begin to change and deliver positive results. **Fulfilled volunteers produce a mission-oriented and irresistible culture of acceptance, friendliness, and fun.** Volunteers who are dialed into their sweet spots are eager to continue volunteering and invite their friends to join them in the experience.

An integral part of helping others find their sweet spot is recognizing the value of roles that are not sweet spots for you. A few years ago, I watched this take place in my church. Our kids ministry director was someone with a friendly, extroverted personality. She loved storytelling, acting, and connecting with families in the hallway. When it came to actors and group leaders, she knew just how to plug them into their roles. Then along came Donna . . .

Donna was a big fan of our kids ministry and appreciated the high-energy environments and small group leaders who made our weekly programming great. But when she desired to get plugged in, none of these roles felt like a good fit. After considering every role we suggested—small group leader, storyteller, host, worship leader—she finally responded with, "I really like making costumes and props. Can I do that anywhere?" Bingo!

Our kids ministry director felt a huge relief as Donna would roll up in her minivan each Sunday and unload robots, costumes, rockets, animals, and all sorts of props to create amazing atmospheres for worship and learning. This behind-the-scenes role provided Donna a massive outlet for joy and meaning, and released our leaders to dive into the relational tasks of recruiting, vision casting, and connecting with families.

The Whatever-You-Need Myth

One of the things we appreciate about Donna is that she did not fall prey to the *whatever-you-need* myth. When we are in a pinch and

STRATEGY 1: CELEBRATE THEIR SIGNIFICANCE

hear a volunteer say this phrase, it can be tempting to trade everything we know about sweet spots for a quick solution. Often when we hear a volunteer say, "Whatever you need," we praise her for her flexibility and availability. Although flexibility and availability are fantastic traits in volunteers, it is our responsibility to not take advantage of an individual who is committed to the mission of our organization.

Leaning into the *whatever-you-need* myth is dangerous because it gives you a false sense of success and sets the volunteer up for potential discouragement filling a role that is not her sweet spot. Letting volunteers choose an attitude of *whatever-you-need* could potentially cause burnout and be the reason they leave your ministry or organization to serve somewhere else.

God fills volunteer vacancies when we honor the people He has entrusted to us. When you fill spots based on your greatest need, people serve out of obligation rather than meaning. Recently a woman who was new to our church stepped up and said she was ready to volunteer. She asked where the greatest need was and I (Christine) refused to tell her. I explained our volunteer process and how before we plug someone into a role, we meet with her to find out about her interests, passions, and background. As I explained our commitment to helping every volunteer discover and continually evaluate their sweet spot, she began to cry. Her previous experience had been at a church where nobody was willing to volunteer in the nursery. The pastor asked her to fill the role until they found someone else. She reluctantly said yes and found herself "stuck" in the nursery for the next ten years. Eventually she left that church because she felt it was the only way to get out of the nursery. After spending some time interacting with our coaching and discipleship process, she now is serving in her sweet spot, and loves leading a women's Bible study and singing in the choir.

It's helpful to have the mentalities that "everything is an experiment" and "nothing is forever." Having these mentalities will provide freedom in how you recruit volunteers and how you engage them within the mission of your organization. When you help people find the perfect fit, instead of simply filling spots, volunteers will stick around!

Make It Count

Think about your own life. Aren't the most memorable moments the ones when someone came into your life and helped you discover what you love to do? As I (Christine) am sitting here writing, I received an email from Sara. She had just moved back to our area, heard about a new ministry being developed, and contacted me to find out how she could get involved. Let me share an excerpt of Sara's email:

> I am currently working at a job as a per diem case manager and I don't like it. I don't dislike it. I am kind of neutral about it. I have been praying to God, asking Him to bring something into my life where I could feel excited and rewarded. I was recently reading a book where the author talked about how he spent so much time doing something that wasn't in line with the gifts that God had given him. He was able to do the tasks needed, but the work didn't really use his gifts. It made me think about why I am not satisfied with my current work position. I realized that the position uses my skills, but doesn't use the gifts God has given me. It uses the things I have learned in school, but doesn't use the things God has instilled in me that cause me to feel rewarded (and I am not talking about financial rewards but that reward that you feel in your soul when you know you are doing what God has created you to do). Some of the gifts I have are leadership, administration, organization, and program development. In some of my previous positions I had the privilege of developing new

programs. I found this very rewarding as I saw things go from the planning, to the development, and finally to the implementation stage. Some people love gardening (and I might too if I didn't kill anything green that comes into my home!); they love seeing the planting of the seed to the sprouting of the plant, to the eventual fruit or flower that the plant shows. That's kind of how I see things like this. It is the way that I think I can put into use the gifts God has given me so I can participate in the growth of His kingdom and that excites me!

As a forty-something, Sara has already had a very successful career in her young life. Her resume is impressive. She holds two master's degrees and has accomplished much by way of climbing the corporate ladder. Yet it is clear something is missing. Sara wants her life to count. She wants her time to count. She wants to be part of something bigger than herself. It is abundantly clear that Sara is looking for significance, and I love that I get to be part of helping her discover her sweet spot. As leaders, this is the most rewarding part of our job!

Next Steps

1. Think about a time that you felt like you were in your sweet spot? How did it make you feel?

2. List the names of five volunteers you are confident are in their sweet spot, and five volunteers you sense are not in their sweet spot. What steps will you take to help?

3 SHOW THE NUMBERS

Elevate the perceived value of volunteers by calculating and communicating their contributions.

Babies and Storks

People measure what they value. Although only a few geek-types admit to loving statistics, the majority of us are interested in our standing, place, and value. We go to sporting events with foam fingers, declaring our team as #1. We plaster car bumpers with honor role stickers. We buy championship jerseys. And we compare the size of our church to others. All of us like to know our value: *Are we first or last? Are we the biggest or smallest?*

Leaders can elevate how volunteers, and others looking in at the organization, perceive the value of volunteer investment by calculating and communicating measurements; such as time invested and what the financial outpouring would be to hire paid staff to fulfill the same roles. Our previous research tells us that showing the numbers is statistically correlated to volunteer retention.

We have all heard the joke that storks deliver babies. In the decade following World War II, it was noted that both human birth rates and the stork population in many western European cities rose rapidly. This caused researchers to evaluate the correlation between the two and come to some conclusions. When the War ended, many families migrated to larger cities. As the population grew, so did birth rates, as well as new construction to accommodate the influx of people. More people equals more buildings. More buildings equals more warm chimneys for nesting. More warm chimneys equals more storks. So in fact, the correlation is not that storks bring babies, but that babies bring storks.

Likewise, as you evaluate your ministry, ask the following question: *Is the work being done by your ministry incredible because you have great volunteers, or do you attract great volunteers because you have an outstanding volunteer culture?*

If you assume that volunteers have nothing better to do than serve within your church or organization, you will tend to be relaxed with timeliness, scheduling, and requests. However, if you understand that every hour of volunteerism is a carefully stewarded gift, then you will appreciate, measure, and leverage time.

Our ability to lose track of the value of an item is staggering. For many years, I (Darren) led leadership development trips for church teams, utilizing wilderness environments as the classroom. It was fascinating to watch the value of common items fluctuate throughout the course of the trip. For example, by the second day in the woods, Fig Newtons were considered worth more than gold. On one trip, I observed a lead pastor offer another leader $20 for his Newtons. As trips would draw to an end, the pain of hiking would begin to fade and minds would drift from smushed Fig Newtons to sizzling steaks on the grill. What was once deemed highly valuable would be forgotten or even thrown away.

STRATEGY 1: CELEBRATE THEIR SIGNIFICANCE

The nutritional value of the Fig Newtons never changed. What did change was their perceived value. Halfway through Day One of the trip, Fig Newtons were like manna from heaven. Yet in the shadow of a grilled steak, the cookies were ditched and forgotten. The point is obvious but painful: **I must never view a volunteer's time as a means to my end, and I must leverage my time as an opportunity to develop him or her.**

The reality is that the volunteers in your ministry aren't *helping* you—they are *saving* you! The reality is you would not see the same level of success without them. Your success is 100 percent dependent upon them and it is crucial that you accept, track, communicate, and value that reality.

Communicating Value

Once you understand the value of your volunteers, you must take the time to tell them how much they matter. Every individual retains information differently, so this is an area where we encourage you to over-communicate. Here are some ideas for how you can communicate their value to volunteers:

1. **Use language to imply value.** Don't forget *people find significance and meaning in knowing they are making a difference.* Words matter, and saying the exact same thing in a very different way can communicate a totally different mindset. For instance, instead of saying, "Thanks, Bob. See you next time," try saying, "Bob, thanks for being here. I love that the guys in your small group are connected, and I can see it making a big difference in their high school."

2. **Use numbers to describe value.** Not every story can be measured. Nobody is bold enough to write, "Our student ministry is 38 percent more godly this month," in their quarterly newsletter. But a lot of what is happening around you can be measured. For instance, you can celebrate that the amount of volunteer time

invested during any given week dwarfs the amount of time paid staff is able to invest. In doing so, you are elevating volunteers as the real heroes—and they love that! Consider a blog heading that reads, "Volunteers provide nearly 70 percent of all personnel hours!" or, "70 percent of our staffing is provided by awesome volunteers!" Stunning headlines like these can be simply calculated by any of your staff (or volunteers!) who love spreadsheets. Consider the following example of a Sunday morning kids program:

> 1 full-time paid staff = 40 paid staff hours
> 15 small group leaders x 3 hours = 45 hours
> 5 host team members x 3 hours = 15 hours
> 5 worship leaders and story tellers x 3 hours = 15 hours
> 5 tech team members x 3 hours = 15 hours

That means that out of the 130 total hours invested in one week, 90 hours are completed by volunteers. That's 225 percent more time than what can be invested by one full-time paid staff!

3. **Use pictures to illustrate value.** Provide a quarterly infographic showing the impact of your amazing volunteers. Consider including items such as the salary value if volunteers were to be paid, total hours invested, and number of staff that would need to be hired to replace them. Not only does this kind of visual raise volunteer morale, but it can also elevate your reputation with your board of directors and financial department.

4. **Use stories to amplify value.** The success of an organization can't always be measured in numbers. Some things can't be quantified, yet hold incredible, eternal value. One of the most powerful tools you can use to ensure volunteers experience feelings of significance is to gather and broadcast stories of life change.

When you take the time to show the numbers, you open the door to two equally important opportunities. The first is for yourself as a

STRATEGY 1: CELEBRATE THEIR SIGNIFICANCE

leader; the opportunity to be amazed by your volunteers! When I internalize that in the past month, 258 individuals left the comfort of their home to invest more than 2,000 hours in families who live in my community, my chest swells with equal parts excitement and responsibility. When I realize that volunteers have given "donations" of time amounting to nearly $50,000 of personnel time, I am incredibly grateful for what is given. When is the last time you opened a letter with a $50,000 donation enclosed? Imagine that donation arriving every week accompanied by smiles and stories of life change. Connecting volunteerism to real hours and real dollars helps me to treat each hour as a valuable gift and prevents me from becoming passive in how I lead that time.

Secondly, a door is opened for volunteers to connect to a larger mission. Showing the numbers communicates to volunteers the role they play in the whole. They will see themselves as an integral part of the team rather than lone rangers. Those who volunteer in behind-the-scenes ways like teardown or building maintenance can sometimes feel disjointed from what is happening. When they are connected to the whole sphere of volunteerism church-wide, they get to see their role as a valuable piece in a much larger vision and team.

Next Steps

1. Go to *https://www.independentsector.org/volunteer_time* and calculate the numbers for your organization. What would it cost in staff dollars to replace your volunteer teams for one week?

2. What are three ways you will communicate the value of volunteers this quarter?

4 CONTINUAL IMPROVEMENT

Be approachable and open, embracing ways to improve processes, communication, leadership, and effectiveness.

Everyone Grows

Growing organizations regularly look for ways to improve processes, communication, leadership, and effectiveness. Those who lead volunteers should continually be evaluating the success and satisfaction of their volunteers, and discovering outlets to help them develop their leadership potential. A commitment to continual development and growth will set your organization apart from other volunteer opportunities.

Our friend and mentor Dennis has the leadership creed *everyone grows*. Dennis is committed to ensuring that everyone around him is on a constant growth curve, even if it means the next opportunity might lie outside his sphere of opportunity. His selfless, open-handed approach to leadership continues to garner massive loyalty. As leaders of volunteers, we need to commit to seeing each volunteer continue to grow, even when the result nudges them to a new volunteer role or threatens our ego.

I (Christine) will never forget the first time I met Jeanette. It was a Wednesday evening, and she walked into the kitchen where I was leading our church's weekly Kids Club. I was in *my* sweet spot and believed God was using me to make a significant difference. I loved what I did so much that I thought I would do it for the rest of my life!

Then along came Jeanette. She was new to the church and wanted to volunteer in kids ministry. As I watched her interact with the kids, I felt a little threatened. She was really good! Maybe even better than me . . . Ouch! The kids loved her immediately and were hanging on her every word. They were fully engaged and eager to do whatever she asked of them. She was younger, hipper, and cooler than I ever was! My first reaction was to get her out of there! I needed to help her find another place to serve, perhaps preschool or the cleaning team. She had moved in on my ministry and needed to be stopped. Don't judge me, I know at some point many of you have felt the same way.

Long story short, Jeanette did not end up scrubbing toilets. Her potential as a leader was undeniable and, after a time of coaching, I passed the torch of leadership to her. She is now a high-capacity volunteer who oversees our elementary small groups ministry of 400 kids and 50 adult volunteers. She has also used her gifts in leading family events and missions trips that have played a part in leading hundreds of kids and their parents to the Lord.

Instead of remaining a threat, Jeanette has become one of my best friends and partners in ministry. I am so thankful I did not let the insecure chatterbox in my brain drown out the voice of God saying I needed to equip others for His work. There was an added bonus that came with helping Jeanette grow as a leader: it allowed me to move into greater capacity in my leadership as well.

STRATEGY 1: CELEBRATE THEIR SIGNIFICANCE

Jikoda and Kaizen

We all think our churches or organizations are great. We wouldn't be part of the leadership if we didn't believe in their vision and potential! However, we can't miss the fact that some organizations are, for lack of a kinder word, better than others. All organizations are in a race for the contribution and attention of a limited pool of volunteers.

It's interesting to note how businesses and organizations generally have the same core mission, similar demographics, comparable volunteer populations, and resources, yet every day they are faced with the challenge of keeping up with the pack. The playing field is generally quite similar, with little differentiation between the "rivals," leaving one to assume each would experience similar results. Yet in every field, there are those who are far ahead of the pack in profits, innovation, scores, and reputation.

In his book *High Velocity Organizations,* Steven Spear describes how innovative, ahead-of-the-pack organizations pursue two ancient and beneficial oriental ideals: *jikoda* and *kaizen. Jikoda* refers to self-regulation and the discipline of stopping immediately when a problem occurs. Prior to producing vehicles, Toyoda (now Toyota) Automatic Loom Works developed a loom that stopped the instant a broken string occurred so as to not ruin the entire bolt of fabric. Prior to this invention, a loom would continue to function despite the broken string, resulting in a damaged product, lost time, and missed opportunity. Stopping a process the moment it breaks or is no longer efficient allows leaders to assess why it broke and how it can be fixed.

The second ideal, *kaizen,* refers to a commitment to continuous improvement. This mindset continues to find better ways to fulfill the desired outcome, never resting on past or current success. Kaizen is the practice of continually learning from the past in order to be better positioned for the future.

In his research, Spear tracks the value of these two principles throughout the US Navy submarine program, steel mills, healthcare, and space travel. In all successful organizations, there was a commitment to identify and deal with problems immediately (jikoda), and to constantly improve processes, communication, leadership, and effectiveness (kaizen). The result is that these companies became leaders in their fields against the odds.

The translation from organizational leadership to volunteerism is flawless. The talented volunteer who values his time will not endure an endless path of workarounds, excuses, and failures; he has high expectations of leadership. The organization that has high rates of volunteer retention will identify the broken systems (jikoda), while doggedly pursuing the next improvement (kaizen).

We do not have the power of the paycheck to overcome our failing approaches or lackluster leadership. Continual improvement is not just about systems, approaches, and strategies. We must provide intrinsic motivation supported by the highest standards of excellence, support, and appreciation. The local church is an institution created and blessed by God Himself, with the most compelling mission, so let us be extremely diligent about removing obstacles that tarnish a perfect plan for impacting the world.

Next Steps

1. What do you need to stop doing in order to rebuild momentum for the future?
2. This week during programming, take notes of what you see broken or needing to be improved. Develop a plan to fix three things prior to volunteers returning the following week.

5 SHOWING APPRECIATION

Focus on praising the gifts and investments of others, and say "thank you" in a way that resonates with each unique individual.

Fill Their Buckets

One of the most significant things you can do to retain volunteers after you have found their sweet spots, showed them the numbers, and committed to helping them continually grow and develop, is to be sure they feel an ongoing sense of authentic appreciation.

We have a tendency to start strong with new volunteers. We are excited to help them find their roles and introduce them to those with whom they will be serving. But sometimes we are quick to move on to the next new volunteer or task, and fail to provide long-term attention to established volunteers. This disengagement is one of the top reasons volunteers quit. They need to be reminded on a regular basis that what they do matters.

Every volunteer has needs that must be met if they are going to invest for the long haul, and one of those needs is to feel genuinely appreciated. Think of appreciation as a volunteer's paycheck. What would you do if you were hired for your dream job, but after a few months, stopped receiving a paycheck? I'm going to assume you might not stay at that job much longer.

Another way to think about appreciating a volunteer is to use the metaphor of filling his or her bucket. Every individual has a metaphorical bucket waiting to be filled with appreciation and praise. When a person's bucket is full, he or she feels valued, and is more likely to be consistent, dedicated, and eager to take on bigger responsibilities.

If you've never read the children's book *Have You Filled a Bucket Today?* by Carol McCloud, grab a copy and settle in to read a simple, yet profound philosophy that will change the way you think about showing appreciation to those around you. The premise of the book is that everyone has an invisible bucket that is emptied and filled, dependent on the things others say to us. When our buckets are full, we feel encouraged and full of energy. When our buckets are empty, we feel down and sometimes even insignificant. Each of us has the ability to either fill or dip into someone else's bucket by the words we say to and about him. When we intentionally take time to fill our volunteers' buckets, we create environments where they feel fulfilled and ready to take on the world.

What's In a Name

For those of us running tight on budgets and time, the idea of a big appreciation bash or expensive gifts can be daunting. The good news is, while these things are great, they are not what matter most to volunteers. One of the top ways volunteers report feeling appreciated is when staff and leaders remember their names and details about their families. In his classic book *How to Win Friends and Influence People,* Dale Carnegie tells the story of a young Andrew Carnegie realizing the power of a name:

STRATEGY 1: CELEBRATE THEIR SIGNIFICANCE

When he was a boy back in Scotland, he got hold of a rabbit, a mother rabbit. Presto! He soon had a whole nest of little rabbits—and nothing to feed them. But he had a brilliant idea. He told the boys in the neighborhood that if they would go out and pull enough clover and dandelions to feed the rabbits, he would name the bunnies in their honor.

Once you've mastered an individual's name, go a step further. Make sure you're pronouncing it correctly. Learn the correct spellings and become obsessive about accuracy when sending personal notes and emails, and publishing lists.

Be Specific

Not only do volunteers feel valued when you remember their names, but they also feel valued when you remember small details about who they are and what makes them tick. Effective appreciation is an art, and in order for it to be impactful, it must be specific and sincere. Praising others for unique traits and actions takes practice. We must learn to be great listeners and find the time to get to know what makes each volunteer unique. My (Christine) friend Debbie is a master at filling invisible buckets. She is especially observant and pays close attention to the nuances and interests of those around her.

One way Debbie shows specific appreciation to volunteers is with an annual Christmas gift. She starts by choosing a theme like candy bars, boxes of cereal, or kitchen gadgets. She then purchases a different item for each person that reflects the individual's personality and why she appreciates him or her. Debbie's volunteer team is small enough that she is able to gather everyone and hand out each gift, while sharing how the item reflects the individual's uniqueness and investment.

For example, one year Debbie gave me a Take 5 candy bar. She said she had chosen it because we have so much fun together. I make her forget about the cares of this world and when she gets to take a break, she loves to take it with me.

Depending on the size of your volunteer team and how much time you get to spend one-on-one with each individual, it may feel difficult to learn and retain details regarding each person. Then when you want to send a card or give a small gift to say *thank you*, you are stuck giving a generic gift card or a greeting card with a cat on the front.

Something you can do to help you be specific when showing appreciation is having new volunteers fill out a brief questionnaire that helps you get to know them better. Ask about things like their birthday, anniversary, favorite way to relax, favorite drink at Starbucks, favorite candy, and their hobbies. Be sure to keep the questions fun and easy to answer.

Once you've collected the questionnaires, keep them in a place where you see them frequently, to remind yourself of unique ways to say thank you. The best part about using this type of questionnaire is most of the time volunteers forget they filled it out. Then when you bring them their favorite caramel macchiato or Peanut M&M's to say thanks, they are blown away by how well you know them. That really makes their day!

Tell Stories

In Chapter 3, we touched on the idea of sharing stories to amplify the value of volunteer investment. One of the most powerful things you can do to ensure volunteers remain focused on the fact that their contribution is making a difference is to collect and celebrate stories of life change. Volunteers don't stick around because of a need; they stick around because of a vision. Stories are proof that the amount of effort they invest equals the amount of change they influence.

Collecting stories sometimes takes a little work. You may know great things are happening around you, but not know how to put a thumb on it. Here are a few ideas to help create a culture where stories are collected and shared:

Provide the tools. Part of creating a culture where stories are shared is making it easy to share your story. Consider providing notecards to those whom your volunteers serve, and ask them to share a story about how they have been impacted. Then have an easy-to-locate place for the cards to be dropped off.

Do a video interview. First-hand accounts are more impactful than a retelling. If you hear about an incredible story you know your volunteers and others should hear, consider asking the individual if they would be willing to tell the story on camera. You can share the inspirational videos on social media or at your next gathering. Don't forget: *What gets celebrated, gets repeated.*

Host a *We Love Our Volunteers* Day. Schedule a day where it is impossible to be in your facility and not know volunteers are a big deal. Get custom T-shirts made and put *We Love Our Volunteers* banners and balloons in your hallways. Hand-deliver special snacks, notes of appreciation, and other surprises.

Keep a file. Even in a culture where stories of life change are shared frequently, we can lose track of what is happening around us. Have specific files in your email and desk drawer for stories. Whenever you are sent an encouraging email or note, treasure it, and store it safely in a place you can easily access later. Then when the time comes for sharing at a volunteer gathering or staff meeting, you will be ready.

We hope this chapter has given you some next steps to take in appreciating your volunteers. As you think about those who serve alongside you each week, ask yourself, "How can I fill a bucket today?"

Next Steps

1. What have you found to be the most effective way to make your volunteers feel appreciated?

2. How can you intentionally make it fun for volunteers to be part of your organization?

STRATEGY 2:
PROVIDE FIRST-CLASS SUPPORT

Effective leadership begins with well-informed and resourced volunteers. Volunteers should be communicated with often and provided tools for their roles in advance. Leaders should invest in training for skills that are applicable in volunteers' homes and workplaces, reaching beyond the roles they fulfill in the church or organization. When this happens, volunteers will exclaim, "I've got what I need and I feel valued!"

6 TRAIN FOR SUCCESS

Have guidelines, policies and procedures, job descriptions, and screening processes in place and be aware of how these elements apply in each specific role.

Being a Student of Others

No one ever told me, "Christine, to be a good leader, you need to be a student of people." I thought I had people figured out because I assumed everyone was wired just like me. I'm a people person, a visionary, passionate, spontaneous, and fun-loving! Unfortunately, this erroneous mentality carried over into the assumptions I made about the volunteers I led. I truly believed that, like me, volunteers were totally cool with last-minute changes and a "Let's just wing it!" approach.

Until one day early in my time leading others, I read a book by Jim Wideman called *Children's Ministry Leadership*. It made me rethink everything! Reading one particular section of the book, I was hit square between the eyes that I had been using my personality as an excuse for not taking time to prepare and properly support volunteers. It was an *Aha!* moment. For a minute, I sat and considered which of my volunteers had told Jim about me. I realized that day that, regardless of my wiring, I had to show value to my volunteers by providing them with proper support.

This realization was reinforced soon after, at the end of a vision casting event with my volunteers. The food was fabulous, we had a ton of fun, and I could not have been more inspiring! At the end of the evening, I was flying high! It was the best meeting ever . . . or so I thought. Then a new volunteer named Tammy pulled me aside and quietly whispered, "Christine, I think I missed something. I appreciate your enthusiasm and passion. I know *why* you want me to be engaged with families. Tonight really was great, but, um, I'm just not sure what it is you want me to *do*. I need direction."

I quickly learned that Tammy is an introvert who thrives on having details. She likes to have a plan and stick to it. Like so many people, she needs direction and clear objectives so she can measure for herself how she is doing. Tammy is a successful businesswoman who owns a dental practice. Her administrative and organization skills are tremendous and I would have lost out on the value she brings to our ministry if I hadn't purposed to make some significant changes in how I lead.

I went into the next meeting prepared with an agenda and a detailed job description for each volunteer. I enlisted Tammy's help in planning the meeting. I listened to her feedback and invited her into the process. I saw the value of a strategic partnership with Tammy, and we were a great balance for each other. Tammy is a behind-the-scenes person that balances my outgoing nature, and our skill sets and personalities combine to create a dynamic midweek program.

To be a great leader, you must know yourself well. You have to lean into your strengths and invite others in to balance your weaknesses. If you want to lead well and retain volunteers, you have to engage *everyone* and not just the people wired like you. By understanding the personalities, learning styles, and gifts of others, you will be better prepared to support, train, and develop volunteers to reach their full potential.

People Over Programs

In our pursuit to fill volunteer roles, we can lose track of the fact that every volunteer is a person uniquely created in the image of God. For this reason, we need to retrain our brains to place people over programs. Jesus called us to do one thing: *make disciples*. It is our job to help others learn what it means to follow Christ because people are our most precious commodity. The reality is that in order to make disciples and lead others, you need to show you value others by planning ahead and communicating early and often.

Keep in mind that a volunteer is so much more than the role they fill. They might also be a parent, a spouse, a student, an employee, a business owner, or a caretaker, just to name a few.

Here are some heart check questions: Does the way you lead volunteers help them to be better followers of Christ? Do they feel cared for and valued by you, or do they feel like just a number? When volunteers leave a meeting or training with you, do they walk away feeling like they are a better parent, coworker, or business leader? Have you added value to their life outside of what they do for your organization?

I hope your answer to many, if not all, of these questions is *yes*. If you answered *no* to any of those questions, you might be thinking, "I do love people, but it's just so hard to find time to provide communication and quality training in the midst of everything else!" I get it, I really do! Perhaps now is a good time to look at the structure of your schedule and prioritize in some key times with volunteers. The health, growth, and discipleship of your volunteers depend on it!

New Volunteer Process

In addition to providing quality training for your existing volunteers, it is also important to think through your orientation process for new volunteers. They need to know what is expected of them and be made aware of their next step. Do you have a clear process for preparing new volunteers to serve in your ministry? Do you keep track of who is in this process so you can expediently help them become fully integrated into your program? Here is our suggested approach for a new volunteer process:

Explore his or her interests. The best part of having volunteer *teams* is that teams are made up of people with varying skills, interests, and experiences. Prior to plugging an individual into a role, spend time getting to know him or her. Find out the individual's preferences on things like being behind the scenes or hands-on, working with people or on projects, and being creative or systems-oriented.

Have the potential volunteer observe in his or her area of interest. It is tough to get someone involved in something about which they know little. Ask the potential volunteer to come observe programming as a guest for one session to see what you do. While he is there observing, have a staff person or coach take some time to chat and find out what the individual is interested in and where he might like to serve.

Provide a weblink to or physical copies of necessary paperwork. Depending on the level of involvement volunteers have with others, especially minors, you will want to have potential volunteers fill out an application and give permission for you to run a background screening. At the very least, you will want to gain new volunteers' contact and basic information so you can contact and celebrate them.

STRATEGY 2: PROVIDE FIRST-CLASS SUPPORT

Complete and approve background screening and reference checks. Again, if you are trusting an individual with the lives of others or your organization's resources, it is wise to ask others if he or she can be trusted.

Welcome your new volunteer to the team and begin orientation. Once you have completed the background screening, reference checks, and necessary office work, you should send an email or make a phone call to say *Welcome to the team!* You should then begin the orientation process. You can do this in an online format, class, or one-on-one setting. We encourage you to keep the information scripted and consistent for all new volunteers. Be sure to include:

- A description of your policies and procedures.
- Expectations for attendance and participation (the frequency in which you need him to volunteer, the start and end time of the commitment, etc.)
- Ministry leader contact info and encouragement to provide feedback and ask questions.

Implement a training process in which the new volunteer shadows you or another experienced volunteer or coach. Just because they filled out paperwork and had a conversation, does not mean a new volunteer is ready to head out on his or her own. Be intentional about providing him or her a mentor, especially for the first month the individual is involved. You might consider doing the following:

- *Week 1*: I Do, You Watch
- *Week 2*: I Do, You Help
- *Week 3*: You Do, I Help
- *Week 4*: You Do, I Watch
- *Week 5*: You Do!

Make intentional contact on weeks 4 and 8. After your new volunteer has been involved for a few weeks, check back in and ask questions like: What do you like best about serving? Is there anything you need to feel more successful? How can I help you?

Check in periodically. People, life circumstances, and roles change over time. For this reason, it is important to check in with volunteers periodically to make sure that what started as a good fit continues to be manageable and life giving.

A clear volunteer process is beneficial for both leaders and potential volunteers. As a leader, you want to know you have the best possible people involved. As a potential volunteer, an individual will need reassurance that he or she has support. This mutual benefit will bring the confidence needed for a successful volunteer experience.

Never Host a Meeting

As you lead volunteers, you will notice items you want to introduce and/or reinforce with your team. You will want to gather your volunteers together in one place to share information, and you may even be tempted to publicize this time together as a *meeting* or *training*. Resist the urge to use these words. Choose something that sounds fun and inviting. We call our volunteer trainings HuddleUP because they pair with our weekly Huddles, which you will read more about in Chapter 8.

The first thing you need to do when planning ongoing training is to **schedule a time.** We hold HuddleUP twice a year, once in the spring and once in the fall. They take place when volunteers are already in the building for regularly scheduled programming. When Christine hosts HuddleUP, other staff and substitute volunteers are recruited to lead programming so regular volunteers can attend the training. Another option is to hold HuddleUP two simultaneous weeks and have half the volunteers attend one week, and the other

STRATEGY 2: PROVIDE FIRST-CLASS SUPPORT

half the next week. This will keep your programming running, in a slightly modified form, and raise the percentage of volunteers who are able to attend this necessary time of fun, inspiration, and information.

The next thing is to **know what you want to say.** One of my favorite voices is that of consultant Mark Brooks, who always says, "A question anticipated is an opportunity seized." When we anticipate what our volunteers are asking or questioning, we have the foresight to seize the moment and provide direct support. Sometimes we expect volunteers to just trust and follow. The reality is your best volunteers will be asking tough questions and will need to understand the answers so they can sync their giftedness alongside your vision.

Once you know what you want to say, you need to **choose whose voice you want volunteers to hear.** In many situations, *you* are the person from whom your volunteers need to hear. You are the one sending emails, dropping notes, and leading weekly Huddles. But if you are making the most of weekly communication and casting vision, biannual volunteer gatherings are a great place to strategically introduce new voices.

Two voices we have seen to be powerful are those of the executive leader and the like-minded outsider. The executive leaders in your organization, such as your senior pastor or president, are poised to affirm, champion, and celebrate volunteers. To have a massive impact, their message does not need to be unique; it just needs to be from them. We would suggest you use an executive leader's voice when your volunteer team needs an extra boost or during times of significant change. Use this opportunity to cast vision for ongoing excellence and augment it with the supportive voice of one of your top leaders.

The voice of a like-minded outsider is exceptionally powerful when you are casting a new vision or desire to instill confidence during the middle portion of a change process. An individual leading through a parallel or similar circumstance communicates to your team they are not alone and there are others championing the same cause for which they are passionate. A like-minded outsider will also reinforce the values you uphold by being another voice saying the same thing. When I bring in an outside voice to speak to volunteers or am acting as that voice, I always initiate a "What do they need to hear?" conversation. This gets the staff leader and the communicator on the same page and helps provide the same-voice experience you desire.

For ideas on how to infuse fun and creative elements into your HuddleUP, keep reading to Chapter 12.

Training Above and Beyond

In addition to your normative orientation and ongoing training, you should offer optional, advanced opportunities for volunteers to gain further knowledge and skills. Many of your volunteers are eager to improve—after all, they are doing this role because they are passionate about it! Giving your volunteers the opportunity to attend a conference or meetup/networking event is a great way to fuel their passion and improve your volunteer team's understanding and skills.

For many years, we have invited volunteers to join us for major conferences and the results were priceless. Think about it for a minute. If you could go online, pay $300, and instantly have a key volunteer position filled, you would do it in a heartbeat, right!? Of course! When you invite volunteers to take next steps in their training, they gain a brighter vision for your organization, a boost in confidence, a new set of relationships, and an injection of *"I matter to this organization!"*

If your budget doesn't allow money for volunteers to attend conferences and meetups, still consider extending the invitation to

STRATEGY 2: PROVIDE FIRST-CLASS SUPPORT

attend. We have had volunteers pay their own way to attend because they are so eager for the training and time together. The invitation itself is a powerful communication of value.

Another way to have volunteers feel a full level of support is to provide them with a free catalogue of resources. This might be a set of online journal articles or links to blog posts you send in their email. You might also have a shelf or resource cart in your volunteer VIP area with books addressing hot topics within the demographic or interest area in which they serve. Relying on like-minded voices who have already created quality resources keeps you from reinventing the wheel and allows you more time to focus on relationships.

Next Steps

1. What are three elements you can implement into trainings that shift people to describing meetings as *fun* and *helpful?*

2. How can you become a better student of people?

7 COMMUNICATE EARLY AND OFTEN

Commit to providing information early, with frequent reminders, so volunteers can adequately prepare for their assignment.

Communicate, Communicate, Communicate

Volunteers play a critical part in completing the mission of an organization. Leaders should commit to providing information early enough for volunteers to prepare for their assignment, with frequent reminders of what lies ahead. Being prepared sends the message that you value people. You value their time, talents, and resources. One way to show you value your volunteers is by communicating with them in a timely and frequent manner. Very few things broadcast your true feelings about volunteers as much as your communication rhythm. Communication that is sent early and is helpful in nature sets volunteers up for success.

When sharing information with volunteers, err on the side of over-communicating. The people who thrive on details will appreciate it and your free spirits will be glad they had the information when the time comes to utilize it. Use a variety of platforms to get the information out—email, phone, text message, social media, etc.

When I (Steph) led small group leaders for middle and high school students, I would encourage the adult leaders to ask their students for the best way to contact them. I was leading at a time when adults were still stuck on email and students had migrated their communication to social media. My leaders were frustrated because students were not responding to their attempts to share encouragement and touch base during the week. It turns out that if students had been inclined to check email, they would have been blown away by their mentors' attempts to reach out to them. But if students didn't check their email, they assumed silence. Our team quickly adopted the mindset that *if your communication is not seen or heard, it is not actually communication.*

The Mike Filter

A few years ago, our team established a principle we call *The Mike Filter*. Mike is a fantastic volunteer with a wonderful family, a successful professional life, and a big heart for people. Mike is a deep thinker and often has questions about programming and event details, the philosophy of why we do what we do, and how we might improve our systems.

It was noted one day in a staff meeting how Mike is more inquisitive than the average volunteer. One member of our team noted how Mike had become the spokesman for probably many other volunteers who were thinking, but not voicing, the same questions. When preparing communication, we began to ask ourselves this question: *What would Mike need to know and when would he need to know it?* If we could empower Mike with all he needed to navigate his busy schedule and his volunteer responsibilities, then we would be able to empower all the other volunteers with the necessary information as well.

Mike is a valued member of our team, and he is too nice to keep asking for more information every time there is a gap. The reality is that if Mike has to beg for the information he needs to perform his

STRATEGY 2: PROVIDE FIRST-CLASS SUPPORT

role, he will soon find another volunteer opportunity that will support him.

Not because he is upset . . .

Not because he doesn't love God . . .

Not because he hates our organization.

No, we would lose Mike because he has a heart for people and a desire to be successful in helping others. He wants to use his time wisely and gravitates toward leaders who partner with him in making a big impact.

If you have not yet identified a Mike on your team, you will want to consider ways to invite feedback from volunteers. Consider using a brief survey or meeting one-on-one or in small groups to ask specific questions regarding how you can best resource your volunteers. All of the volunteers in your ministry have opinions and ideas, so make sure you welcome and invite their feedback as often as possible.

Establishing a Communication Plan

Volunteers need to be communicated with early. They need to be communicated with often. And they need to be communicated with consistently. Establishing a regularly occurring schedule for communication gives your volunteers confidence they will know what they need to know, when they need to know it. Effective communication plans include details for the immediate and a brief heads up for what is coming in the future.

Your communication plan should include multiple layers. Consider mapping out a yearly calendar with a sequenced approach to ensure your volunteers receive the right amount of communication for each layer at the appropriate time. Work with your team to coordinate communication incorporating special events and

HuddleUP topics. Your layers should include some of the following:

Weekly. Each week, provide information relevant to the immediate volunteer experience. Answer the question: *What do I need to know before arriving this week?*

Upcoming. This information is perfect at the beginning of a new month, as an overview of upcoming events and reminders. Answer the question: *What should I be planning for and thinking about?*

Values. This foundational information is well-timed quarterly, at the start of a new season or celebrating wins that have taken place over the past 3–4 months. Answer the question: *Why do we do things the way we do?*

Motivation. Even when a volunteer understands the core values of your organization, it can be difficult for him to internalize the power of his individual role. Answer the question: *Why am I still doing this?*

Training. A wise leader keeps his eye out for things like blog posts, podcasts, and videos that will benefit his team. Supplying one resource each month that takes volunteers 5–10 minutes to listen to, read, or watch can be a helpful reminder and simple way to equip volunteers. Answer the question: *How can I do this better?*

Transitions. This information is sent out on an as-needed basis. It addresses strategic and urgent changes and is often done best in person or with plenty of opportunity to interact and ask questions. Answer the question: *Does this upcoming change make sense?*

Last-Minute Changes. All leaders make last-minute changes from time to time. As much as possible though, try to limit the occurrence of last-minute changes. Changing plans can often be an inconvenience and, when done frequently, can lead to frustration and mistrust. Also keep in mind that when you change things too

STRATEGY 2: PROVIDE FIRST-CLASS SUPPORT

often, it can send the message you are incompetent. Making a habit of communicating at the last minute sends the message, "I care about me." Communicating early and often sends the message, "I care about you."

Next Steps

1. When do you communicate with volunteers? *Be sure to consider when communication* actually *happens, and not the communication* plan.

2. Who is your Mike—which volunteer provides input as to what issues and information you need to address?

8 WEEKLY HUDDLES

Set aside time immediately prior to programming and events for volunteers to gather for final instruction and coaching.

Huddles

When volunteers arrive for an event or program, it is highly beneficial to gather everyone for a volunteer Huddle a few minutes prior to start time. One would never expect an athlete to jump in the game without warming up first. In the same way, wise leaders set aside time immediately prior to programming to gather volunteers for final instruction and coaching. Let me tell you why we call them Huddles—they are designed to be missional, brief, team-focused, and to launch volunteers into action.

We would suggest having volunteers arrive thirty minutes prior to start time, so you can allow ten minutes for Huddle, five minutes for final prep, and your team can be in place fifteen minutes prior to the start.

In addition to providing connections, Huddles also provide opportunities to clearly communicate who is the go-to leader for volunteers. Volunteers appreciate knowing who is in charge and connecting face-to-face with a real person. Having access to a staff person or established leader gives volunteers confidence, the ability to ask questions, and someone to communicate with when a need arises. People are more prone to give suggestions or ask questions of someone they know truly cares.

Head, Heart, and Hands

Everyone arrives at Huddle coming from various places and still processing their day. Huddle is a great way to redirect thoughts and emotions toward the volunteer experience. It can mean the difference between success or failure. Significance or waste. Confidence or doubt. When you plan for Huddle each week, a rule of thumb is to provide something for your volunteers' heads, hearts, and hands.

Head: What do you want them to know? Huddle isn't the place for lengthy announcements or outlining curriculum for the next year, but it is a great time to give reminders, inform about upcoming events, and share details about that day's programming.

Heart: How do you want them to feel? Share a brief story of a win that unfolded the week or month before.

Hands: What do you want them to do today? Confirm they have the tangible resources they need to get the job done. Make sure they have enough of the worksheets, tools, and Krazy glue necessary for the project.

Tips for a Successful Huddle

Like we said before, Huddles are a brief, yet integral time with volunteers. The following are a few tips for running a successful Huddle:

Give a friendly welcome. As volunteers arrive, be ready to welcome them with a smile, high five, or even a hug. Let them know where they can grab a snack or find the bathroom. Give them a heads up as to where they need to be at what time by saying something like, "Good to see you, Kelly, thanks for coming! We will get everybody rolling for the day by huddling in the lobby at 9:00 a.m. sharp."

Be present. When your volunteers arrive, be ready for them. Once volunteers are in the building or programming space, you should be finished with personal tasks and focused on mobilizing them to be successful. The presence and preparedness of leadership communicates that volunteers are valued and important members of the team.

Start on time. We all hate showing up only to stand around and wait. You know that moment, when everyone stands around exchanging awkward glances, wondering if anyone is in charge or prepared. It can be tempting to delay until all of your volunteers arrive, but this may communicate to those who arrived on time that their time is not valuable. Delay a few weeks in a row and you will begin to notice your volunteers arriving later and later. Be consistent with your start time and volunteers will become consistent with arriving on time.

Keep it short. Huddle is meant to be a stand-up meeting that lasts ten minutes at most. Keep your announcements, stories, and last minute details short. You may choose to end Huddle with a brief prayer. Prayer is an important element that draws people together; however, keep in mind that opening the floor for prayer requests may extend the length of time in Huddle. Effective leaders may want to consider alternative options for providing a community of prayer support outside of Huddle.

You will also read about Huddles in the section on fueling meaningful connections because we believe these times together are crucial to the retention process. People need community, and even just one friendship can influence a volunteer to leave or stay involved in your ministry. It's important to create environments where people experience opportunities to connect with other volunteers. To read more about the social benefits of Huddles, keep reading, or even flip to Strategy 3: Fuel Meaningful Connections.

Solo or Off-Site Volunteers

Many organizations have support teams that serve in groups of one to three people who serve off-site or during non-programming times. These could be people who help maintain your facilities or prepare weekly resources. Not all volunteer roles are created to foster a Huddle environment, but keep in mind that your goal is to ensure all volunteers feel known, supported, and connected. In order to do this, you will need to develop a system that greets, informs, resources, appreciates, empowers, connects, and supports—all while not relying on your constant, physical presence.

An exercise that I (Darren) often do to force myself to lead outside of physical presence is what I call the "cast scenario." What I do is imagine I have had a horrible accident and find myself bed-ridden with two broken legs. Then I begin to ask myself, "How can I lead today from this hospital bed? How can I mobilize, encourage, and empower others?"

This exercise helps me to step outside the constraints of physical presence and begin to think in terms of outcomes. It helps me to remember I am not held accountable for checking off tasks. I am held accountable for ensuring I take care of the most important things in the best possible way.

In order to support off-site or solo volunteers, consider questions like the following:

- How can I let this volunteer know I am thinking about them?
- What would make this group of volunteers laugh?

STRATEGY 2: PROVIDE FIRST-CLASS SUPPORT

- What is a special treat I could leave in their supply closet for when they arrive?

You can communicate appreciation and presence through simple actions like the following:

- Send a text a few hours before their scheduled time.
- Leave candy or another treat at the place they check in.
- Drop by and take a selfie with them, then Tweet about their awesomeness.
- Host a monthly meetup at Starbucks for those who serve at unique times (don't forget to pay for the coffee!).
- Schedule a team member to stop by while they are serving, say hello, and make them laugh.
- Find out their coffee/tea drink of choice, and have their special orders delivered.

Developing an organization where all volunteers are supported, from the most public roles to those serving behind the scenes, creates a place where people choose to stay invested. Take time this week to appreciate each unique volunteer position, from the most public roles to those serving behind the scenes.

Next Steps

1. If you don't already hold a weekly Huddle, circle a day on your calendar when you will begin.

2. Do your volunteers who serve during non-programming times feel supported and appreciated during the week?

9 MAKE IT SAFE

Have measures in place that protect the volunteer, participant, and families within your ministry context.

A Sigh of Relief

For those of us wired relationally, and who find ourselves to be naturally trusting of others, the idea of policies and procedures can seem like a drag. Not everyone is wired to always be thinking about rigid guidelines. Yet as we interact even with young ministries or small-town churches where everyone knows each other, we implore leaders to establish well-known policies and procedures to protect the children, families, and volunteers in their organization.

Consider the following story. Although it is difficult to tell, it has played out in hundreds of churches with sometimes positive and at times tragic results.

One afternoon, a church receives a heart wrenching phone call. It is from an individual accusing one of the church's kids ministry volunteers of abusing him ten years prior. He is calling the church to let the leadership know he will be pressing charges, and is concerned that others may also come forward as victims.

The volunteer being accused is one of the sweetest, kindest, gentlest people the ministry knows. The kids and other volunteers love him. The heart of the leader receiving the phone call begins to pound out of his chest and tears begin to flow, as his mind starts spitting out one questions after another. "This can't be true, can it?" "How could we not have known?" "What if it is true and he did hurt one of our kids?"

The leader takes a deep breath and begins to think about their kids ministry's long-standing policies, procedures, and best practices. Prior to serving, this man had been screened for a criminal record and other legal violations. Because of the strict policy that no volunteer ever be alone with a child, this man was never unsupervised. The church has security in their hallways and glass windows on all of the doors. Volunteer coaches are always nearby, checking in on the classrooms periodically. As he remembers all the parameters set in place that would prevent a volunteer from secretly harming a child during programming, he feels himself begin to breathe again.

When you are short on volunteers or in a hurry, it can be tempting to stray from your policies and procedures. Compromises are tempting when you are under the gun. It can be easy to let your guard down when you are busy or dealing with chaos. But let me encourage you to keep making it safe, so at the end of the day, your leaders and volunteers can serve confidently.

Mr. Safety

I (Darren) have at times been mockingly called *Mr. Safety*. To others, I seem obsessed with release forms, seatbelt safety, and outsourcing recreational activities to professional outfitters. I laugh along with the jokers, but inwardly I think, "Mr. Safety! Really!? But I enjoy whitewater kayaking, rock climbing, and off-road racing. One of my hobbies is welding. I even ride a motorcycle!" The truth is that something larger than safety is important to me. What I am

STRATEGY 2: PROVIDE FIRST-CLASS SUPPORT

really concerned about is the mission. I am all about the mission God has invited us to be part of and nothing will derail the pursuit of the mission more than the consequences of negligent behavior.

An awesome worship set is ruined when one kid lands on her head while crowd surfing.

> An impactful missions experience is forever tainted by an accusation of sexual misconduct taking place on the trip.

> > Attendance numbers plummet when parents do not feel confident with the driving skills and behaviors of the volunteer leaders.

I am convinced that paying attention to safety and following best practices frees me from distraction and ensures I stay focused on the mission. The kids and adults in your care are important to God, and I bet you would rather push your mission forward than deal with the massive distraction of legal action. What you do is too important for the divergence that comes from 911 calls, ambulances, and lawyers.

Keep in mind that life change, not safety, is the goal. But as leaders, we have an obligation to lead well and avoid as many distractions as possible. A few issues that must be addressed as we engage volunteers are the following:

Screening. The more responsibility a volunteer has, the more stringent your screening process needs to become. The screening for a small group leader of minors should be significantly more involved than the process for someone interested in helping with data entry. An appropriate process for a high responsibility volunteer (this includes all who work with minors) will include an application, interview, criminal background check, confirmation of identity, and possibly a waiting period.

Training. You must identify the key things a volunteer needs to know, feel, and do in order to adequately fulfill his or her role. Anything less is setting both of you up for certain conflict or misunderstanding.

Insurance. Prior to implementing volunteer roles within your organization, be sure you have specific coverage in place so that volunteers can have confidence the organization will support and protect them in case of any issues.

Supervision. Supervision is a must because evaluation, affirmation, feedback, correction, and possibly even termination are all mandatory jobs for those who lead volunteers.

Vehicles. Transporting others, especially minors, can be especially tricky. We encourage leaders to recruit dedicated drivers when transportation is local and reasonable, and hire professional drivers whenever possible. Some best practices for transporting others are to limit the vehicle's capacity to the number of working seatbelts, not ask anyone to drive more than six hours, restrict caravanning, provide every vehicle with directions and a phone, and to have zero tolerance for careless or reckless driving.

Stupid games. During our combined decades of interacting with volunteers, camps, churches, and social agencies, we have repeatedly been amazed at how even seemingly mature, responsible leaders will revert to inane behavior when it comes to games and pranks. Unfortunately, many of the "amazing" games and pranks of our youth are actually downright stupid, unsafe, and demeaning. Just because your pastor loved games that stuffed marshmallows down kids' throats when you were a kid, doesn't make it wise. It was a choking hazard then and it still is today. You should define for your volunteers what is appropriate in the realm of games and jokes in accordance with what supports the mission. I never want a student to be nervous to attend an event because they might get hurt or be the brunt of a joke.

STRATEGY 2: PROVIDE FIRST-CLASS SUPPORT

Protection. Volunteers should be made aware of how they need to provide protection for the population they serve. In order to ensure emotional and physical safety, they may need to do things like enforce the check-in system in their classroom, redirect conversation from bullying, and stay alert and observant during events. A volunteer's commitment to these matters will be directly tied to your personal commitment to them. If you as a leader are slack, sloppy, or sarcastic, then your volunteers' actions will be magnified versions of your poor behavior.

Industry Standards and Other Risk Management Principles

Not only do the children and families in your care benefit from policies and procedures, but they are equally valued by your volunteers as well. When a volunteer learns there are safeguards in place that protect not only families but also volunteers, he is extremely grateful. In Urban Institute's study of 3,000 charities, the top 25 percent, with the most volunteers giving the most hours, had best practices related to policies and procedures in place. From this, we can infer that organizations with clearly structured and communicated guidelines in place have a higher rate of retention among volunteers.

As a leader, it is your responsibility to train and inform volunteers on the policies and procedures of your organization. It is important to understand that in most states, volunteers are held to the same standard of care as paid staff. A parent or participant is expecting a professional level of care for themselves or their child regardless of the person's employment status with the organization. It is not acceptable to assume that a lesser standard of care will be applied to someone just because she is a volunteer. Be sure to read the following sections carefully, and do your research to find out how each principle applies in your particular location and ministry setting.

1. Industry Standards

You are brilliant—and so are many other people who do what you do! In fact, lots of creative, insightful people have been doing what you do for decades. Over time, many lessons have been learned. The wisest practitioners quantified those lessons and communicated them to others through conferences, associations, journal articles, and textbooks. These sets of learnings have been compiled to create an informal but powerful set of standards known as *industry standards*. These standards are not laws. They are not moral issues. They are simply compilations of wisdom.

A wise leader taps into industry standards in an attempt to move her mission forward more quickly without having to pay the stupid tax. When it comes to safety and liability, industry standards and best practices will be the measuring stick by which you will be judged. If you follow current industry standards, then there is a good chance the best expert witnesses in the business would testify on your behalf in the event of legal action. If you ignore best practices, then the same expert witnesses will be testifying against you in the court proceeding.

Take the time and energy to become aware of your wider circle of industry or ministry so you are informed of the constantly changing landscape of safety and liability. You may even consider reading texts on leisure, recreation, and sports law to gain a better understanding of the issues surrounding group programming and volunteer liability.

Recommendations:

- Ensure your volunteers are leading activities and events in a manner that meets or exceeds industry standards.
- Send volunteers to be trained and certified to lead certain types of activities that are deemed as high risk.
- Provide volunteers with manuals, checklists, and best

STRATEGY 2: PROVIDE FIRST-CLASS SUPPORT

practice explanations.
- Review, inspect, and improve your policies and guidelines at regular intervals.
- Help volunteers to understand the separation between personal hobbies acceptable as an individual, but not appropriate with a group trusted to their care.
- When participating in activities your insurance does not cover, such as rock climbing or paintball, transfer the risk to a professional organization certified in that activity.

2. The Doctrine of Foreseeability

The doctrine of foreseeability pertains to whether an activity or product could cause a negative, predictable incident. In other words, can the average person foresee if the item or activity could lead to harm. For instance, could someone foresee that placing forty high school students on one piece of playground equipment for a photo may cause it to collapse or that the fourth car in a caravan may have to run a red light to stay with the group.

For those who work with minors, it is important to view programming through the lens of the participants. Being fully engaged in leading programming helps prevent boredom. If not given clear direction and supervision, participants may choose other, less-than-safe alternatives.

Participation in a community of industry experts through conferences and associations helps you to gain insight. Purposefully inviting others to observe your programming or event will also provide valuable wisdom. You may even consider inviting input from law enforcement, first responders, colleagues, and parents.

Recommendations:
- Participate in your community of industry professionals through conferences, meetups, and reading articles and

blog posts.
- Encourage volunteers to be deliberate and wise in their actions. Prepare your leaders by helping them think through, "If this . . . then that . . . " scenarios.
- Be fully prepared and engaged when leading programming or an event.

3. Mandatory Reporting

Many staff and volunteers are bound by state law as mandatory reporters of child abuse. It is critical that you understand your state laws on this matter. Not only should you understand the laws, but you must also have appropriate procedures in place so volunteers understand what they are to do if an issue surfaces. Be prepared for the sake of the families you are committed to serving. Clearly train your volunteers on policies, expectations, awareness, reporting, and prevention.

Recommendations:

- Ask your insurance company to provide training to your staff and volunteers.
- Before establishing them in place, have all policies reviewed by a lawyer who specializes in nonprofit law.
- Build solid relationships with your county's child services office.

4. Risk Management

A commitment to safety is a commitment to responsibly managing risk. Obviously you cannot avoid all risks, but the wise leader clearly understands when additional care needs to be taken. In teaching risk management classes, I (Darren) address issues like risk transference, equipment and facility inspections, and supervision. My hope is that you take a class, pursue some learning, or invite

STRATEGY 2: PROVIDE FIRST-CLASS SUPPORT

experts to assist you and your team in areas of risk management pertinent to your ministry situation.

Recommendations:

- Read *Better Safe Than Sued* by Jack Crabtree.
- Know and communicate the guidelines outlined by your organization's insurance company.

Disclaimer: This chapter provides general guidance about a variety of complex legal issues. It is not a substitute for legal advice. Laws vary from state to state and change often. Therefore, readers are urged to consult a local attorney regarding their particular context, policies, and trainings.

Next Steps

1. When is the last time your policies and procedures were reviewed by your insurance company? *Our suggestion is to have this done annually.*

2. What steps have you taken to ensure your volunteers feel safe and protected?

10 ORGANIZING VOLUNTEER TEAMS
Establish an approach to structure volunteer teams and educate volunteers on leading other volunteers.

Growing Your Team

Properly caring for and supporting volunteers is no easy task. It requires time, energy, and resources that are in short supply for busy leaders. We would imagine that if you're reading this book, it is not because you sit around twiddling your thumbs looking for something to do to kill time. If you are reading this book, you're a busy leader who is looking for effective ways to find and keep great volunteers who will help carry the load. At times, you may even feel a little overwhelmed and like you're in over your head. We've all been there.

In fact, if anyone can relate to that feeling, it's Moses—and he's one of the greatest heroes in the Bible! Moses was on an incredible mission but, at one point, he was also on the brink of burnout. He was the epitome of trying to be all things to all people and in Exodus 18, Jethro, Moses' father-in-law, offered him some great advice that all leaders should take to heart.

From morning to evening, Moses would listen to and help solve disputes among the people. And from morning to evening, people would stand around waiting to have their cases heard. Jethro counseled Moses: "*What you are doing is not good. You and the people with you will certainly wear yourselves out, for the work is too heavy for you;* **you cannot handle it alone**." Jethro then gave Moses some great advice on delegation. He advised Moses to lighten his load and maximize his impact by selecting qualified, honest men to appoint as leaders over smaller groups of people. Then Jethro closed with this thought, "If you do this… you will be able to share the strain and all of the people will go home satisfied."

You will share the strain *and* the people will be satisfied. Wow! Take a deep breath and say those words out loud. I don't know about you, but there are days that I feel like leadership is tough. Some days, I just don't feel like there is enough of me to go around. I feel like I'm being pulled in a million different directions and I can barely keep my head above water. I get so busy accomplishing tasks and checking things off of my list that I forget the real reason why I'm doing what I'm doing. Tasks are necessary and the work needs to get done, but we need to be careful to always put our volunteers above our programming.

That is why as your ministry grows, you will need to increase the size of your volunteer teams. The key component to growth is ensuring that all volunteers feel the care, connection, and support they need to stay fully engaged in your mission. You will want to continually ask the questions, "Does everyone feel connected to someone?" and, "Is someone caring for each volunteer?" As your number of volunteers increase, this task becomes more challenging. The need for a second tier of leadership becomes imperative.

Take a moment to consider what it looks like when one leader becomes overwhelmed by too many volunteers, and things like communication begin to break down. It is important that communication be received from someone with whom the volunteer has a personal relationship. We are convinced that . . .

If a volunteer receives an email from an anonymous someone in the office, he will miss the personal connection.

> If a generic card is delivered and obviously filled out by the church secretary, a volunteer may wonder if you are outsourcing your care for her.

>> If appreciation gifts are delivered by mass mailing with no personal note, you may foster a culture of cynicism.

Thinking through how to structure your volunteer teams in a manner that leverages personal relationships helps each person to feel a personal connection. We are strongly convinced that you can grow your team by resourcing high capacity volunteer leaders. Yes, you can have teams of volunteers who lead teams of volunteers.

Another benefit of a well-structured team model is the ability for volunteers to easily access help when they need it. Volunteers will feel far more secure if they know who their go-to person is and who has the knowledge and authority to "get it done." Regardless of your structure, every volunteer should know who is his or her contact person. This person should be accessible and ready to provide help. Long-term retention of volunteers requires we eliminate dark holes of confusion and fill them with clarity, communication, permission, and resources. The highly supported volunteer is a long-term volunteer.

Volunteer Coaches

The important thing to remember when structuring your volunteer teams is to leverage relationships and help each volunteer feel a personal connection. We are convinced that you can grow your team by developing a second tier of leadership with high capacity volunteer leaders. We call this level of volunteers who lead teams of volunteers *coaches*.

We recommend mobilizing one coach for every ten volunteers. A ratio such as this ensures that communication, encouragement, and care happen in a personal way. That means if you have fifty volunteers, you will want to have five coaches who will each oversee and provide care for ten volunteers. These numbers don't have to be exact, but we have found that organizations that have a healthy volunteer culture are those that strive to provide close to a ratio of one coach to ten volunteers.

In the corporate world, Disney is a master at providing over-the-top care for their employees. They recognize that no matter how effective the CEO and other executives are, it is virtually impossible for them to effectively care for and mentor all of their team members. So they assign one coach/team leader to a small group of employees. Sound familiar? The coach's role is to provide localized care and mentoring for his or her small group, to help them succeed both in their staff roles, as well as in life. Disney's top leadership believes that every person is worth the investment. If Disney can do this, our organizations can too!

In Ephesians 4, Paul explains how God gifted *us* to lead so that we can *prepare and equip* God's people for works of service so that the body of Christ may be built up. This means that we're not supposed to do all the work ourselves; we're to train and lead volunteers to do the work of God. The word *prepare* comes from the Greek word *katartismos*, which means perfecting or preparing fully. This refers to a process that leads to full preparation. It's about intentionality. A leadership development process doesn't just haphazardly happen. It needs to be well thought out. It requires a plan.

STRATEGY 2: PROVIDE FIRST-CLASS SUPPORT

Writing a Job Description

When Jethro advised Moses to select qualified, honest men to appoint as leaders over smaller groups of people in order to make his load lighter, he was teaching him a valuable lesson about the power of delegation. The art of delegation comes by first identifying the job description of a potential volunteer coach. The next step is to identify the person. It's really no different than hiring a staff member. Once you have written a job description, then write a list of core competencies for the position. This should happen before you set up interviews with potential candidates.

In order to write a job description for a coach, start by asking the following question, "If I had more time, what would I do better in the areas of providing care for, showing appreciation to, and supporting my volunteers?" Give yourself permission to dream a little. Once you know the answer to this question, write it all down in the format of a job description.

Now that you are clear on *what* it is that you would like for a coach to do, it is time to consider *who* you should ask to join the second tier of your team. Writing a job description before you identify a potential coach makes the process of recruiting that person much easier. Don't make the mistake of saying, "Hey! I think you'd make a great leader here in our organization. What do you think of that?" If they are a great leader, they're going to come back with the obvious question, "What does that look like? What are you asking me to do?" If you're smart (and we already know you are), you will have taken the time to think it through and be able to provide a well thought out, written job description.

To get you started, here is an example of a job description from one of our volunteer ministries:

THE WIN FOR CONNECT TEAM COACHES

As a coach of the Connect team, we need you to care for, manage and communicate with your volunteers. You win when the Connect team members feel known, trained, and celebrated so they can make first-time guests feel welcomed and appreciated.

ACCOUNTABILITY

- Team Leader: _____

QUALIFICATIONS

- You love God
- You care about Connect team members and the first time guests with whom they communicate
- You are committed to managing, training, and communicating with the Connect team members for at least one year

RESPONSIBILITIES

- Make sure your team members are known
    - Connect with them regularly
    - Be aware of major events and needs in their personal lives and communicate those to Connect Team Leaders

STRATEGY 2: PROVIDE FIRST-CLASS SUPPORT

RESPONSIBILITIES CONT.

- Make sure your team members are trained
    - Facilitate weekly team Huddles to ensure that volunteers feel empowered to answer questions and assist first-time guests. Be sure to highlight important details and last-minute changes
    - Hold monthly parties/trainings to review your guide process
    - Communicate and encourage Connect team members to attend parties/trainings and other team events
    - Attend the appropriate training events and meetings to be prepared to train and meet with the team members you lead
    - Check in with your team members quarterly and ask evaluation questions that aid in training and updating procedures and systems
    - Host new volunteer "test drives"
    - Pray for team members
- Make sure your team members are celebrated
    - Ask each team member to share their wins with you
    - Relay stories to Connect Team Leaders
    - Encourage them through regular and random notes, emails, and encouraging words to let them know that you notice the great things they do
    - Celebrate birthdays, anniversaries and milestones

The 5 C's of a Coach

In addition to knowing what you would like for a coach to do, you also want to focus on who he or she is as a person. When we are attempting to identify a coach, we look for volunteers, often within our current volunteer teams, who have the 5 C's: Character, Conviction, Competence, Commitment, and Chemistry.

Character. When choosing a coach, look for volunteers who have a proven track record of being reliable and trustworthy. You can impart a skillset, but character and integrity are more difficult to teach. Does the potential coach have a clear understanding of what it means to follow Christ and is there evidence of that in his or her life? Does he or she have a teachable spirit?

Conviction. It is also important to look for volunteers who uphold the mission and vision of your organization. Do they value people and appreciate how they are uniquely wired? Do they see potential in people?

Competence. You're looking for someone who has a proven track record of being responsible and coachable. You want to know they not only have ability, but availability as well. Are they willing to take on more responsibility? Be careful not to make the assumption that someone is too busy. Busy people get things done.

Commitment. Look for volunteers who are committed to God, to the volunteers in your organization, and to you as their leader. You're looking for someone who has your back, is a team player and a servant leader. They are respectful of the system, but may challenge the process—great leaders always do. Are they committed to excellence and open to evaluating experiences without taking things personally?

Chemistry. Do yourself a favor and give this one the weight it deserves. Chemistry is crucial! Is the person's personality a good fit for your volunteer team? Does he embody the DNA of your organization? Is he humble and cooperative? Is he an encourager? Is he relational?

Choose Wisely

Take your time when transitioning a volunteer to the level of coach. We recommend that before you speak to someone about being a coach, you give him or her small, incremental opportunities to lead. Give her tasks related to pieces of the job description to see how she does, and then provide feedback and coaching to see how teachable she is. For example, ask if she would lead Huddle or assist with your next volunteer training by sharing a devotion or story.

The reality is it's hard to fire a volunteer. It's not impossible, but definitely difficult, to say the least. Spend time in prayer asking God for wisdom and guidance as you identify and develop new coaches. Then get ready for your job to get a lot easier as you invest in a few, who will in turn invest in their ten. The effects of this model are indescribable in more ways than one. Your volunteers will begin to receive the support and encouragement they need to succeed in their roles and you will receive the blessing of watching people develop into their God-given potential as you teach and model biblical leadership.

Kellie is a perfect example of this. She was a volunteer who was quiet and unassuming, always serving behind the scenes. Her first leadership role was a huge stretch for her because it required her to interact with a lot of people. I later learned that for the first few months, she would literally get sick before coming in to serve each week. But Kellie has a desire to invest in other volunteers, and with a little bit of coaching, she has developed into an amazing leader of leaders. She now coaches other coaches, adding another tier of leadership in our organization.

Kellie was given opportunities to coach and lead because she encompasses the 5 C's. She loves a challenge and she's eager to learn and grow! In the past two years, she's read too many leadership books to count, has become an avid listener of leadership podcasts, and has even become a leadership conference junkie too! As a result, she is now one of the strongest leaders in our organization who is duplicating herself by consistently developing new leaders. The added bonus for me is that because Kellie is the complete opposite of me (Christine), she's become my wingman and together we've been able to accomplish so much more than we could have ever done alone!

Just like I have with Kellie, when you commit to structuring your volunteer teams in a manner that leverages relationships and helps each volunteer feel a personal connection, you will reap the rewards on multiple levels. And when you're tempted to do it all by yourself, remember Jethro's advice to Moses when he said, "If you do this . . . you will be able to share the strain and all of the people will go home satisfied."

Isn't that what it's all about? Volunteer satisfaction equals volunteer retention!

Next Steps

1. Assess the number of volunteer coaches needed to provide adequate support and care for your volunteers by dividing your total number of volunteers by ten.

2. Write a job description for coaches and begin to pray about who God would have you begin to develop as a second-tier leader.

STRATEGY 3:
FUEL MEANINGFUL CONNECTIONS

Many people choose to volunteer because they are looking for community and connection to other like-minded people. This strategy focuses on team building principles and the importance of providing opportunities for volunteer groups to share stories, play, and laugh together. A volunteer experiencing community will express the sentiment that, "I belong here," and "I've got friends here."

11 FRIENDSHIP-FRIENDLY PROGRAMMING

Develop environments where like-minded individuals can connect and grow together.

Created for Community

In the book of Genesis, we read the account of creation. God created man, and as He steps back to admire His creation, He says that not only is it good, it's, "Very good." Yet shortly after, God declares it's "not good for man to be alone" and He creates a companion for Adam. We're relational beings who crave community. We were born to partner together to do great things for God. It's all part of His design.

In Chapter 1, we discussed how volunteers desire to feel like they're making a difference, an idea that researchers refer to as *participation efficacy*. In this section, we'll discuss how not only do people desire to make a difference, they desire to make a difference alongside others. Research shows one of the main reasons individuals choose to volunteer is the opportunity to develop new relational connections. Volunteering opens up a wide relational world—like connecting with other volunteers, staff members, and those in the community being served.

THE VOLUNTEER PROJECT

In Abraham Maslow's hierarchy of needs, Maslow describes belongingness to be one of the major needs associated with human behavior. The need to belong is an intrinsic motivation to affiliate with others. Our need to belong is what drives us to seek out stable, long-lasting relationships. It is what draws us to participate in social activities such as clubs, sports, teams, religious groups, and community organizations. By belonging to a group, we feel as if we are part of something bigger and more important than ourselves.

Welcome to the Team

I (Christine) didn't grow up in the church. For the first year and a half of attending as an adult, I simply observed, feeling completely inadequate to engage in ministry. I didn't know a whole lot about what it meant to be a Christian, let alone what it meant to volunteer. I had no training, no experience, and no real connection to others in the church. But I wanted to be part of something bigger than myself, and I wanted to have fun and make friends! Life was hard and I needed the support of friends. I had a husband and three very busy boys who were nine years, two years, and six months old. I was a busy mom running two demanding businesses and carrying enough stress to sink a ship. Yet I was craving to be used by God to make a difference and as I watched volunteer teams having fun together, I longed to experience that same camaraderie. *I wanted to belong.*

The church and faith-based organizations can offer to people what very few organizations can: deep meaningful relationships. You can provide for one of people's deepest desires: authentic friendship. Knowing where to find new friends is a challenge for many adults, and volunteerism is tailor-made for helping build friendships. It removes the awkward moments and provides meaningful activity. The dreaded "will they invite me again" feeling is replaced by a weekly or monthly commitment. The opportunity to try new roles provides for additional pools of relationships.

STRATEGY 3: FUEL MEANINGFUL CONNECTIONS

Our friend Stuart Hall says, "You don't choose your friends, they choose you." In other words, friendship is driven by an invitation far more than a pursuit (that's called stalking). Volunteer teams extend an ongoing invitation: *Would you like to join us next week?* Remember, volunteers do not volunteer, they simply say yes to an invitation.

Two Motivators: Obligation and Satisfaction

As leaders, we have a clear idea of the gaps in our volunteer needs. Far too often, we assume people volunteer because they want to help fill our open spots. As nice as this would be, it is a myopic and misguided understanding of what motivates a volunteer to volunteer.

In his book *Fusion,* Nelson Searcy explains there are two things that help individuals feel connected to a church: relationships and responsibilities. In ministry settings, we often fall into the trap of believing people should volunteer for the sake of the mission or because Jesus told them they had to serve. We call this the motivator of obligation. **Obligation** depends on reminding volunteers of their duty to do for others because of what has been done for them. Obligation is characterized and fueled by guilt.

Volunteers motivated by obligation will get the job done but they will not develop a culture that is attractive to new volunteers. Volunteers motivated by obligation may be viewed by leadership as having higher levels of servanthood, maturity, and humility. While these are excellent traits to possess, they will not draw in new individuals looking to be involved. A volunteer culture motivated by obligation often results in high turnover and disappointment.

As a leader, you have a choice to make when it comes to what motivates your volunteers. You can choose the motivator of obligation, or you can lean into the motivator of satisfaction. **Satisfaction** depends on providing meaningful connections and first-class support to volunteers. Satisfaction is characterized by opportunity.

Jesus modeled this well. He came to earth as the Son of God. When it came to recruiting the twelve disciples, He could have leaned into obligation. Instead He spent years building meaningful relationships with them—praying with them, partying with them, encouraging them, teaching them, and my favorite, breaking bread with them. He told fascinating stories and asked controversial, thought-provoking questions, drawing them into deeper community with Him and one another. I really believe this is what made them stick by His side when life got crazy and times got tough. *(Okay, quit judging. So there was a time or two when they got a little scared and hid, but I'm not convinced I wouldn't have done the same considering the circumstances.)*

We believe the act of serving is beneficial for the person. However, we can not confuse theology with leadership. Here's what we mean: We must teach and call people to biblical values, but we must lead in light of their human condition. For most people, the driving motivator to volunteer is not driven by sacrifice or humility. We must lead and manage with this reality in mind so we can assist them on their journey toward growth. The volunteer wants a relational connection with other people. At some time in the future, she may point to serving as assisting her in her spiritual and emotional journey, but for a prospective volunteer, the focus is on the question, "Will I make new friends?" So let's build our volunteer opportunities as places where community happens.

When you focus on community, your volunteers' commitment to the mission will follow. Satisfaction turns obligation into devotion. Wise leaders develop environments where like-minded individuals can connect and grow together. Volunteers have already done their job by saying yes to the responsibility. It is now the role of the leader to help them build relationships; to help them experience meaningful community.

STRATEGY 3: FUEL MEANINGFUL CONNECTIONS

A Place to Belong

Like anything worth doing, creating community requires *intentionality*. It doesn't happen automatically. We can become so consumed with programming and our weekly to-do list, we fail to see the importance of connections.

Brinda came to my church like many people do—burned out. After getting to know her over the course of several months, I asked if she would be interested in volunteering. As the question left my mouth, Brinda's face filled with sheer panic. She explained how at her previous church, she had volunteered for several years in roles nobody else wanted to fill. She had been motivated by the feeling of obligation and served alone in roles nobody else wanted. I told Brinda I was committed to helping her find a volunteer opportunity that would fulfill her tremendous potential, and spent some time just getting to know her better.

It was not long before Brinda came back and said she would like to begin serving. When I asked her what caused her to change her mind, Brinda said she really wanted to make friends and be connected to others. About a year later, Brinda was walking through some extremely difficult family situations. Wanting to be sensitive to her needs, I asked her if she needed to take a break from volunteering, and was blown away by her immediate response:

> NO WAY! These people [her fellow volunteers] are what keep me going! They are my support system. They are the ones who pray for me each week and have made meals for my family. Sometimes they even love me and support me better than my biological family. I don't know what I would ever do without them. I'm not going anywhere!

Brinda experienced a community that compels volunteers to remain in their roles. Providing people with meaningful relationships and a place to belong brings value to their whole lives. We were not created to be alone. Isolation is dangerous. Please don't misunderstand me. I am not saying community keeps individuals from struggle or heartache. But community does provide a circle of care, prayer, and support. These types of connections are what draw volunteers together and propel them forward for the long haul.

So how do you create community? How do you help volunteers engage in friendships that foster healthy community, people sharing life together, and enriching one another's lives? Keep reading to find out.

Next Steps

1. Are your volunteers motivated by obligation or satisfaction?

2. What opportunities do you provide for volunteers to connect?

12 MAKE IT FUN!

Seek to make the volunteer environment fun and a place where volunteers enjoy coming to serve.

Creating a Culture of WOW!

Several years ago, my (Christine) team hosted our annual planning retreat for our kids ministry staff and coaches. We began the weekend like we do every year: by evaluating the previous year. This year was exciting because we had so much to celebrate! When it came time to discuss areas we would like to improve, we even felt great about the quality of our programming and curriculum. As we sat and pondered what we might want to improve, we realized that our need wasn't in the tangible areas of WHAT we do or HOW we do it, but was in the intangible reality of WHO we are being while we interact with volunteers and those who attend our programming.

We were missing the WOW! factor. After a lot of hard work and prayer, we left the weekend with a clear plan for how to create a WOW! experience for every volunteer and family that entered our environments. And we knew that for this to happen, we would need to incorporate a spirit of fun and playfulness.

In order to create a WOW! culture, you have got to find ways to make the volunteer experience fun, creative, and spontaneous. Fun and playfulness have been shown to decrease stress, increase retention, aid communication, and boost energy levels and cooperation. As adults, many of us have forgotten how to have fun and tend to take ourselves too seriously. On the flip side, fun is natural for children, who laugh about 400 times a day, compared to the average adult who laughs 15 times a day.

Having fun is about helping people to take what they do seriously while taking themselves lightly. For many of us, the nonprofit or church ministry we lead *is* serious business. We have a critical, life-changing mission and we want our staff and volunteers to lead with maturity and vision. Creating a WOW! culture means helping others to enjoy each other while still maintaining a spirit of professionalism and respect.

It's important to remember many of our volunteers already have jobs where they spend the majority of their waking hours. The last thing they want is another boring job *at your church or organization!* So make their volunteer experience fun and help them build meaningful friendships. Volunteers who are having fun and building strong relationships are the ones who will stick. Added bonus: They may even invite more volunteers!

Jesus Had a Sense of Humor

Leaders should seek to make their volunteer environments a place where people enjoy coming to serve. Most of us shy away from draining relationships and gravitate toward friendships that are life giving. As you lean into fun, you may need to give yourself permission to craft a culture marked by laughter, lightness, and appreciation. Far too often, churches and nonprofits can inherit the misconception that in order to serve God, we must be serious, maybe even suffering. At Orange, we like to say that *fun over time*

STRATEGY 3: FUEL MEANINGFUL CONNECTIONS

equals connection. It's in the shared experience of laughter that we visibly show we are connected and actually like each other.

Don't forget, God is the author of fun! We believe with all our hearts that Jesus was a fun guy to hang out with. He was the one who said, "Unless you become like little children, you will not enter the kingdom of heaven." I picture Jesus hanging with the disciples, cracking jokes, breaking bread, laughing, and purposely creating moments of tension that would make others cringe. Can't you just picture the disciples' faces when He would sock it to the Pharisees? I can see Him with thousands at His feet, teaching timeless truths through the use of stories relevant to everyday life. He was fun and creative, and excelled at making every moment an unforgettable WOW! experience.

We fully believe every individual is gifted to do something amazing, and when in his or her sweet spot, his or her demeanor will be marked by joy and happiness. Think about how attractive it is when you see a group of people having fun together. Doesn't that make you want to join in! The families and individuals who enter your halls will know if volunteers are serving out of obligation or satisfaction. If they like what they see, they may even be compelled to see how they can get involved too. So go above and beyond to ensure your volunteers are in a role that gives them life, joy, and satisfaction.

Less Meetings, More Parties

Have you ever wondered why people don't show up to meetings and trainings? The answer is simple: *meetings are boring!* The word *meeting* is synonymous with bullet point lists and agenda-driven monotony. Next time you gather volunteers, consider calling it something other than a meeting or training. Call it a *party* or come up with a creative name. But if you change the name, you better do your best to make the time feel different than a regular 'ole training. Volunteers will only fall for that trick once!

So what makes a great volunteer meeting not feel like a meeting? Here's a few key ingredients you can consider to implement fun into your next time together:

- Include items like coffee, munchies, and dessert.
- Have contests. Give away prizes.
- Play team-building games.
- Intentionally decorate the room in a way that tells volunteers, "We knew you were coming."
- Cover the tables with paper so people can doodle and write down their creative ideas.
- Tell stories of life change, celebrating volunteers who are knocking it out of the park. Keep in mind: *What gets rewarded, gets repeated.*

Next Steps

1. What are you doing to ensure your volunteers laugh each week?

2. What area of your ministry has the least amount of WOW!? Gather your team to brainstorm ways to add some fun in your environments.

13 PLANNING CONNECTIONS

Connect each individual with a person who will mentor him through the orientation process and welcome him with a caring and engaged spirit.

Three Connections

When integrating new volunteers, every individual should be connected with a person who will guide them through the orientation process and welcome them with a caring and engaged spirit. In a way, leaders should be matchmakers, uniting new friendships among volunteers. New volunteers should be connected to three individuals or groups: (1) a staff person who cares about them, (2) a coach or mentor to guide them, and (3) a peer group volunteering alongside them.

Connecting to Staff

Research shows that volunteer satisfaction increases when the individual feels a connection to staff. This doesn't mean every volunteer should have coffee with the lead pastor or president of the organization, but it does indicate the importance of every volunteer feeling a level of friendship or connectedness to at least one staff person. They may only see that staff person once a month, yet being connected with the name and face of a real person makes volunteers feel more secure in their role.

In healthy volunteer organizations, staff in every division is mindful to connect potential volunteers with their area of interest, and not just the one he or she leads. Often in an organization, the first staff person an individual meets is not the person who will be working alongside them in his or her volunteer role. A team-playing staff person is a savvy connector of people and ensures volunteers are cared for and led well by introducing volunteers to other leaders.

Our friend Mark has a magnetic personality. Everyone is drawn to his friendly demeanor and big smile. Mark led the adult ministries at the church in which I (Darren) led the family ministries. I would often see Mark coming down the hallway with a new acquaintance, eager to introduce him or her to our family ministries staff. Mark cares deeply for others, and is aware that he can't be everyone's best friend. He knows the success of a volunteer is dependent on the individual having a strong connection to the leader overseeing the program area where he or she serves. Mark's selfless approach fostered a healthy volunteer culture organization-wide.

Here are a few ideas of ways leaders can help volunteers in their sphere of influence feel connected to staff in their organization:

- Provide encouragement by sending a handwritten note to all volunteers in your sphere of influence.
- Schedule coffee meetings. Use this time to get to know your volunteers on a personal level, but also to ask open-ended questions like, "Tell me some of the reasons you enjoy volunteering," and "Is there anything I can provide to resource you better in your role?"
- Pop into programming areas to say hello and give high fives. Invite other staff in your organization, particularly those in executive leadership, to do the same.

STRATEGY 3: FUEL MEANINGFUL CONNECTIONS

- Remember details like the name of their spouse and children. Ask questions about current life events like goings-on at work or in family life.

Connecting to a Coach or Mentor

It is normal for new volunteers to be filled with questions and maybe a little nervousness. Taking on a new role can be intimidating, and it is our job to ensure we give volunteers the gifts of answers and encouragement. Volunteers need a person in the room, across the cafe, or down the hall who can guide them through those first weeks and onward. Depending on the size of your organization, you probably use slick web tools like Planning Center™ to schedule volunteers, which volunteers love. Yet in a world of email and auto replies, it is crucial that volunteers have a go-to person to text or call when they have a question or something comes up. They need a personal connection with someone focused on their area of programming.

Since it is not possible for you to be the go-to person for every volunteer, we would encourage you to recruit volunteer mentors for your programming areas. We call this next tier of leadership a coach. A coach is your eyes on the area, knowledgeable and ready to connect volunteers with answers to their questions and encouragement for their roles. A coach is a high-capacity volunteer, consistently present and committed to helping other volunteers win. For more information about coaches, refer back to Chapter 10.

If you want your coaches to be successful in leading other volunteers, you will need to model for them the way you hope they will lead volunteers. Spend time with them, invest in them relationally, listen to their thoughts and concerns, and praise their successes. You might even consider an annual one-day retreat or weekend planning getaway when you brainstorm, cast vision, celebrate wins, show appreciation, and just have fun together.

Building a culture of community among your coaches will help them experience the value of team and reproduce it among the volunteers they lead.

Connecting to Others

Effective leaders think in terms of connecting and networking others to each other.

Do you remember the emotions coursing through you at your first middle school dance? What it was like to walk into a room and be unsure of the cultural norms. The agony of wondering if anyone would want to hang out with you. The worry about if your dance moves would look goofy, or if your feet would even make it to the dance floor! Keep in mind the emotions of a middle school dance, and commit to never sending your volunteers out on the "dance floor" alone.

When I walk into a programming area with a new volunteer, the first thing I do is introduce him or her to the three friendliest volunteers in the room. Your top three will be the people who love getting others involved. They are the ones extending invitations to others to hang out. In the sentiment of Kid President, they don't go to parties, they *are* the party.

In our early years of church ministry, my wife Becky and I implemented a strategy for connecting people we call *The Buffet Strategy*. As programming was winding down, we would start saying to everyone we saw, "We're headed to Golden Corral™. Who else is going? Are you coming?" By the beginning of the meal, a small group of us would have gathered around the table. We would leave an open seat in the middle of the group for the new volunteer to sit in, leaving ample opportunities for conversation and new connections.

As we talk about this desire for friendship, we need to be reminded that our culture is becoming increasingly segregated by generation and age. A value we can bring to our volunteers is to connect them with a wide range of generations, experiences, and backgrounds. Research shows that an individual's commitment to faith is highly improved by the presence of multi-generational relationships.

Dr. Chap Clark, of Fuller Theological Seminary, lobbies strongly for the value of every high school student being engaged with five mentors. Likewise, in my years as a family pastor, I observed the impact students have on adults to keep them grounded, relevant, and young.

Multi-generational friendships are powerful for all ages. Without purposeful interactions with young people in their lives, adults begin to believe the myths that young people are reckless and disengaged. Without the input of experience, young people miss out on wisdom and guidance to grow and mature fully. Diversity fosters a healthy, balanced experience for everyone.

Next Steps

1. Which of your volunteers do you recognize as natural connectors of people?

2. Draw your volunteer structure. Does it look like a pyramid or a flat line?

14 GET IT ON THE CALENDAR
Set aside regular times for volunteer training, team building, and appreciation.

In the busyness of weekly programming and regular events, simply completing mission-critical tasks can fill the schedule of even the most balanced full-time ministry leader. In this chapter, we want to focus on the importance of setting aside regular times for volunteer training, team building, and appreciation.

Some aspects of education and appreciation happen naturally in the course of the volunteerism assignment, however, many of the important elements will not. It is imperative to have a training and appreciation rhythm that aids volunteers in feeling equipped and valued. A quality training plan will connect them to a wider group of volunteers, provide opportunities to celebrate the contributions of others, and give a platform for staff to celebrate wins.

Organizations with excellent volunteer cultures seem to have some similar patterns for training and appreciation. Here are some common ones:

Weekly Attention. As you walk into your programming areas and observe volunteers, open a note on your phone or tablet and look for specific stories you see of volunteers doing things right. That week, send them a handwritten note or email, praising them for their investment. Try using a format like: *Dear [Name of Volunteer], thank you for your investment in [Name of Ministry]. This week I noticed you [Describe Specific Scenario] and I want to tell you it made me feel so [Insert Elated Emotion of Choice]. I'm so glad you are part of our team. See you next week!*

Monthly Emphasis. Do something simple each month to say thank you. Consider a random giveaway paired with a story of amazingness, or having key staff members walk through your programming area saying a quick yet sincere, "Thanks for what you do!" Nothing says, "You rock!" like a high five from someone you respect.

Biannual HuddleUP. Twice a year, host a short meeting during normal volunteer times to focus on vision casting, training, and overall development. By doing your HuddleUP during regular programming hours, you can raise participation by 90 percent. You can go back and read more about HuddleUP in Chapter 8.

Annual Appreciation Bash. Throwing a party specifically to honor volunteers is a great way to show appreciation and have fun together as a group (for more on this, check out Chapter 12). This is the event for which you pull out all the stops. Spend time and energy planning the event. Invest budget money and resources to make things extra special. Invite your executive leadership to come serve hors d'oeuvres or sing a parody song. The presence of top leadership sends a huge message of affirmation and value. We have thrown parties inspired by cruises, game shows, famous locations, award shows, and more.

Annual Focus. Having an annual emphasis week on volunteerism goes a long way in elevating the importance of people getting involved in the mission of your organization. Not only does it let those not yet involved know about volunteer opportunities, it also elevates the importance of current volunteers. If you are leading within the context of a church, sharing testimonies from the stage, having volunteers wear special T-shirts, and highlighting the value of how serving raises rapport and invites others into your story. Often this launch is coupled with an orientation that allows new volunteers to get up to speed quickly and smoothly.

Next Steps

1. Who do you need to network with to get appreciation events on the calendar? (*Executive leadership, teammates, etc.*)

2. Of the five items you need on your volunteerism calendar, what one or two things could you get on the calendar in the next month?

15 COMMUNITY CAN BE MESSY

Know how to embrace conflict and facilitate the resolution process for future growth.

Tension is Good

Whenever people work together in teams, there is potential for disagreement or conflict. A skilled leader knows how to embrace conflict and facilitate a growth opportunity for everyone involved. Think for a moment about the times in your life when you grew the most and experienced God's presence in a powerful way. It probably was not a time when things were perfect and without bumps in the road.

Many people run from conflict because they believe that by avoiding conflict, they are being more like Jesus. But when we read the New Testament, we can learn a thing or two about the power and effectiveness of tension. Think about how Jesus used tension as a catalyst to teach, unpack truth, and deepen and strengthen relationships.

In a blog post from several years ago, Reggie Joiner said it this way:

> He partied with tax collectors and prostitutes—to challenge the disciples' deep-rooted prejudices.
> He broke sacred traditions—so they would value people.
> He led them into a stormy sea—to take away their fear.
> He angrily interrupted a church service—to expose how greed can corrupt leaders . . .
> He publicly debated religious leaders—so He could clarify what really mattered.
> He didn't always explain what He said—so they would wrestle with what He meant.

The lessons Jesus taught His disciples through tension gave them perseverance and zeal to complete the mission. It's not easy to embrace tension, but it is beneficial. If we want to fulfill the life-transforming mission to which we have been called, it is going to take passion, determination, and even some tension.

Tension Must Be Managed

While tension is a good and necessary part of growth, it must be managed. One of the most important roles of a leader is to monitor and adjust the volunteer culture. If your volunteer culture begins to sour, then your recruitment and retention rates may fall. Commit to observing and listening to the volunteers you serve alongside. Ask yourself questions like: What is the vibe? Is this a fun environment? Are there volunteers others avoid? Are there unhealthy cliques developing?

There will be times you need to go outside your own observations and ask your volunteers for feedback. You should listen patiently and carefully weigh each response. You may receive negative feedback. You may hear things you don't like. But you have to deal with it. Here are some principles to help you manage tension:

STRATEGY 3: FUEL MEANINGFUL CONNECTIONS

Do your homework. Set your team up for success by doing the hard work of screening, interviewing, training, and observing new volunteers. Get to know potential volunteers so you can help them find their sweet spot. Be inquisitive. Be patient. If you notice a volunteer is in the wrong role, remove or reposition them immediately.

By keeping someone in the wrong role, you are choosing for others to leave. There is no "I" in team, but the failure or success of your volunteer team could come down to one person. If you notice a lack of trust or see people scrambling to cover the mistakes of one person, address the situation immediately. Your volunteers are amazing, dedicated people, but they will only deal with this type of frustration for so long. One lousy volunteer, or even a fantastic volunteer in the wrong role, could cost you dozens of other volunteers. Be observant. Be fair. Be direct.

Assess if this is a lousy volunteer or an awesome volunteer in the wrong role. It can be uncomfortable to initiate a conversation with a difficult volunteer. But you must either initiate an hour of uneasy dialogue or suffer through months of discontentment, backbiting, and pain. Through the conversation, you may find out this is an awesome volunteer who hasn't yet found their sweet spot or you may find this is a volunteer who no longer agrees with the mission and vision of your organization. A team member who is no longer on board with the direction of your organization may spread his or her opinion to others and continue to breed discontentment. Committing to address issues quickly will prevent discord from growing wider. Be speedy. Be clear. Be loving.

Keep in mind your credibility as a leader is determined by whether or not you will make the tough decisions in a timely manner. Failing to solve an issue can quickly overturn the positive volunteer culture you have built. One caustic volunteer. One moldy room. One broken but critical piece of equipment. Make a practice of regularly asking yourself: Is there a person, item, or policy undermining the culture and mission of this organization? If so, address it quickly. Be brave. Be decisive. Be tender.

Accept all feedback as a gift. Some of your volunteers will offer suggestions and criticism with grace and maturity. Others will deliver feedback in a way that feels like dropping a sack of bricks on your big toe. Remember that even though an individual might be inappropriate in how they provide feedback, you must still hear and evaluate what he or she says. Even the most unpleasant criticism could hold at least some truth. The good news is the quicker we address and resolve issues, the less likely it is a team member will become caustic. Be approachable. Be a listener. Be humble.

Those are some tough, but necessary, principles if you are going to create environments where people love coming to volunteer and attend. I remember when I had to "fire" my first volunteer three weeks before my official day on staff at the church. One of the current directors shared with me about a volunteer who was sabotaging the experience for the entire group of children she led in a small group. The director explained there was not a moral issue or safety concern, but kids no longer wanted to attend the program because the volunteer leading the group was "mean." Leaders had come alongside her and coached her on interacting with that particular age group, but the negative buzz among parents and other volunteers continued.

As the new guy, it was a tough conversation. (*Heck, it would have been tough as the old guy too!*) But within a few weeks, that small group found a new leader who was gifted in interacting with children and the program was back to its former level of excellence. When you enter the mess, go armed with grace and love, knowing that a few minutes of pain can pave the way for future satisfaction.

STRATEGY 3: FUEL MEANINGFUL CONNECTIONS

Observation, Interpretation, and Clarification

Something we have learned and taught our staff teams is to always think the best of others. When you work with people on a regular basis, it can become easy to prematurely judge their intentions or read into their actions. One of our favorite tools for entering the mess and treating others with positive emotion is called OIC (or "Oh, I see!"). It was developed by our mentor Dennis Wilhite, who is a pro at treating people with respect and leading through the mess.

OIC starts with an **observation.** You notice a behavior or situation that makes you uncomfortable or violates your organization's policies and procedures. After taking a moment to consider the environment, you form an **interpretation** of the situation. Finally, you ask the individual for **clarification** regarding what you observed.

You begin with a non-emotional statement of an observed fact, follow with your possible interpretation of those facts, and end by asking the individual to clarify their actions. Here's what it may look like:

> *Leader:* Hey, Susan, I noticed during small group time, when you normally would be leading the kids, you were focused on your phone instead. That made me think maybe you were interacting with someone or dealing with a pressing matter?
>
> *Susan:* Yeah, actually my grandma was admitted to the hospital last night. I was texting with my mom to figure out travel arrangements and next steps.
>
> *Leader:* Oh, I see, that sounds really tough. I appreciate you being here with all that going on. Would you like me to find someone to help cover your group so you can step away and sort that out?

Or . . .

> *Leader:* Hey, Susan, I noticed during small group time, when you normally would be leading the kids, you were focused on your phone instead. That made me think maybe you were interacting with someone or dealing with a pressing matter?
>
> *Susan:* Actually no, everything is fine. I just am not sure how to talk to kids that age and sometimes get bored during small group time.
>
> *Leader:* Oh, I see! Would you be willing to have someone come alongside you and help you learn how to better lead children? Or would you possibly want to explore other serving opportunities?

In either case, you were able to treat the individual with compassion rather than contempt, and now have the information you need to either resolve a personal issue or provide further training and encouragement.

Next Steps

1. Is there a tough situation you have been avoiding? If so, why?

2. What issue(s) do you need to address in order to foster healthy community?

Bonus: For additional resources on conflict management, check out the book *Boundaries Face to Face* by Cloud and Townsend, and Andy Stanley's podcast titled Trust vs. Suspicion.

STRATEGY 4:
EMPOWER THEIR PASSIONS

This strategy focuses on establishing clear vision and parameters within volunteer teams. If leaders do not give clear vision, volunteers will invent their own. Empowering volunteers happens when leaders remove the red tape and give volunteers permission to carry out the mission. We challenge leaders to not make assumptions for their volunteers, but invite individuals into opportunities that will stretch them beyond what they have done in the past. Volunteers will be excited to say, "I'm trusted and have opportunities to develop into a better leader."

16 INVITING WITH INTENTIONALITY
Be specific about volunteer needs and describe how each unique individual could play a part in completing the mission.

Monster Myth

Before we go any further, there is something we need to clear up. There is a misguided idea floating around that we need to set straight. The myth is this: *Volunteers volunteer.* Buzz. X. False. Nope. Research clearly shows that the vast majority of individuals who volunteer did not volunteer just to volunteer. On the contrary, they were invited, tricked, or badgered into volunteering by a friend or acquaintance. (*Please note:* We do not advocate tricking or badgering potential volunteers.)

Unfortunately, many of us who depend on volunteers can be fooled into believing help will just show up. Then we are disappointed when volunteers don't just walk in our doors. The longer we hold onto this myth, the deeper we dig ourselves into disillusion. A belief that volunteers volunteer is what causes us to preach on the virtues of commitment and character, instead of improving our volunteer culture. It is this belief that makes us louder and bolder instead of more relational and caring. It is why we dangle "free donuts" instead of crafting experiences that fuel intrinsic rewards.

Busting this myth and acknowledging that **volunteers don't volunteer** introduces you to a fresh world of hope and opportunity. You are no longer held back or controlled by the actions of others. You are free to create and build an experience that is irresistible. You can develop a volunteer culture you will be excited to invite others to join, confident they will have a great experience. All you have to do is ask.

The Perfect Ask

I (Darren) grew up the son of a college professor and coach. I vividly remember him correcting the flawed statement "practice makes perfect." He would softly but confidently say, "No, son, **perfect** practice makes perfect." Practicing correctly while paying attention to the details leads to continual improvement and is a strong value of winning coaches.

When trying to recruit new volunteers, we can often think that practice makes perfect. Unfortunately, we can believe that results come as a matter of percentages; that if we make enough asks, we will eventually get enough volunteers. While there is a low level of validity in the idea that even a blind squirrel finds a nut every now and then, there are far better ways to recruit quality volunteers.

Great leaders have learned that their ability to have a great volunteer culture is highly tied to how good they are at making the right ask. Volunteers don't volunteer. They respond to a compelling ask that invites them into a bigger story.

If practice does not necessarily make perfect, then simply asking someone to volunteer does not guarantee a positive response. A sloppy ask could lead an individual to say no to the opportunity.

STRATEGY 4: EMPOWER THEIR PASSIONS

Inviting individuals into your mission will take more than just asking. It will require asking the right way.

Everyone Makes Assumptions

The best asks are linked to the leader's knowledge of an individual's interests and passions. A good leader practices listening skills and engages others in conversation about who they are and what they do. They make the ask with a simple phrase like, "Wow, that's a fascinating hobby! Have you ever considered sharing those skills with a group of students? Our team would love to tell you more about ways you could share those skills with others." This type of ask sounds more like an invitation than a request for help because you are offering the individual an outlet for something he is passionate about. When inviting volunteers to join a team, leaders should be specific about the need and describe how the unique individual can play a part in completing the mission.

Sometimes we make faulty assumptions about why people should serve in our ministries. Without learning about their background or interests, we apply nonsensical reasons to why we think people should volunteer. We say things like, *"Your kiddos are here, don't you want to spend more time together!?"* or, *"Don't you think it is your duty to serve here since your family attends?"* Maybe you have even said this one, the king of guilt asks, *"If we don't have more volunteers sign up, we will have to cancel programming next week. If you love kids, please volunteer now."*

While listening takes energy and time, it is worth the investment when you have the opportunity to connect a potential volunteer with a role that excites him. As we said in Chapter 11, nobody gets excited to volunteer when motivated by obligation. Practicing engaged listening skills shows people you care and will raise your recruitment and retention numbers.

Another assumption that gets in the way of making the right ask is believing people are already clearly informed regarding your organization's vision and needs. You might even wonder why people are not as excited as you are about the opportunity to volunteer in such great roles. The reality is that people may have a misunderstanding or two about your need. Let's consider a few common reasons people express for not volunteering:

"They have plenty of help." It is true that you do not want your ministry to appear desperate for volunteers. This can cause people to either volunteer for the wrong reason or stay away because of what may appear like a non-satisfactory environment in which to volunteer. However, be open when you are looking for new volunteer team members by saying things like, "If you enjoyed tonight's program and would like to be part of the team, we would love to talk to you!"

"They wouldn't want my help." Highlighting unique roles and celebrating leaders' stories are fantastic ways to express that everyone's help is needed. Consider interviewing current volunteers about how they use their individual skills and abilities to serve others, and share the stories in your blog posts, newsletter, and other communication tools.

"I'm too old," or **"I'm too young."** Purposely recruiting a wide range of volunteers will strengthen your teams and expand your potential volunteer pool. Take time to explain why you recruit those who have tons of life experience, as well as those who are just getting started.

"I'm not qualified." How you describe volunteer roles will determine if people feel qualified to fill them. When you write job descriptions for volunteers, do so in a way that laymen and people outside your circle of expertise can understand. Let potential volunteers know you will provide resources, training, and ongoing support to help them win.

**"I want to do something meaningful and that looks like it is

STRATEGY 4: EMPOWER THEIR PASSIONS

all fun and games." If your programming is centered on children or students, we hope it looks like you are having a ton of fun! But don't forget: *volunteers want to make a difference.* When you cast vision to potential volunteers, talk about all of the fun, but don't forget to highlight ways your programming or organization is making a difference in the lives of those involved.

"I want to volunteer, but I really need to help myself right now." Most of us feel the need to be involved in activities and pursuits that improve our overall wellbeing. Be strategic in spotlighting volunteers whose volunteer role has added value to their lives outside your walls. My friend Jeanette is a perfect example. For several years, Jeanette has had the opportunity to communicate publicly to groups of people through her role as a volunteer. She was recently asked to speak at a professional conference through her job and received feedback that she was the best facilitator at the conference. Jeanette called me when she returned home, to say thank you for the on-the-volunteer-job training she had received. In addition to being invited to speak at future conferences, her employer also offered her a promotion with a nice, big raise!

"It's too big of a commitment." Yes, some will shy away from a large commitment, but research actually shows that retention and satisfaction are correlated to the size of a commitment. A large commitment and big ask communicates importance and value, which seems to increase volunteer retention.

"But I have kids." Make it easy for those with kids to volunteer, and communicate how volunteering can position parents to be even more prepared for the future. Depending on the makeup and needs of your organization, consider ways you might provide childcare for young children whose parents volunteer. Also consider how multi-generational serving opportunities can be filled by multiple age groups, provide shared experiences, and engage entire families together.

Group Asks and One-on-One Conversations

Strategically leveraging your organization's communication platform can grease the wheel for a positive one-on-one conversation. Utilizing resources that cast a wide net creates a culture where wins are celebrated and volunteering is the norm.

Organizations with great volunteer cultures have carefully crafted an ask that resonates from the main stage, written communication, special events, and social media. Engaging your organization's communication team to develop a *we love our volunteers* mentality sets your team up for success.

Telling stories is one of the most powerful ways to recruit volunteers. For example, during one of our weekend worship gatherings, we shared the story of a volunteer named Doug. He is a Vietnam vet who began a ministry to feed homeless veterans in our local community. The video told stories and shared pictures of those who were homeless, as well as told Doug's story of why he does what he does. At the end of the video, Doug simply said, "I need help." His story paved the way for great follow-up conversations with potential volunteers.

Roles and Attributes

The most effective asks connect individuals with roles that are congruent with how they see and define themselves. As potential volunteers respond to a group ask, consider both the specific **roles** available and the **attributes** you desire. Some times you need to ask for a specific role to be filled, such as a parking team member. Other times, you need to express the need for a specific giftedness (also known as an attribute), such as the ability to provide clear directions to others.

STRATEGY 4: EMPOWER THEIR PASSIONS

Roles are fixed titles, typically linked to external skills and interests. Examples of roles are:

- Guitar player
- Sound technician
- Accountant

Attributes are the personality and character traits that make individuals tick. One particular attribute can apply to a variety of roles. Examples of attributes are:

- Artist: looking to express and create
- Handyman: eager to fix, repair, and build
- Teacher: zealous to share knowledge and insight
- Administrator: organized and great at delegating
- Helper: enjoys selflessly assisting others and meeting needs

When you raise the value of both roles and attributes, you are then positioned to help every individual find the perfect role. A well-led team of individuals with varied attributes will always get the job done.

Next Steps

1. What systems do you have in place to ensure an individual can find a great volunteer opportunity in his or her sweet spot?

2. Is there someone on your volunteer team being under-challenged? How could you expand his or her leadership opportunities?

17 SET THEM FREE

Cast a crystal clear vision so you can spend less time managing people and more time accomplishing your organization's goals.

Disappearing Act

For a number of years, I (Darren) had what felt like a revolving door of great volunteers. My best volunteers would get off to a blazing start but then disappear after a season or two. It was the worst feeling. I would just finish praising their amazingness to other team members, build plans with them in mind, and then *poof* they were gone. After this happened a couple of times, doubts began to creep in and I became discouraged.

Then while listening to a speaker at a conference, a light bulb came on inside my head. The communicator said that *volunteers need a clear vision and the freedom to carry it out.* I sat up in my seat and began furiously scribbling notes in the margin of my notebook. Mystery solved! I was holding on too tightly to my opinions and way of doing things, and quenching my volunteers' abilities to carry out their gifting. They felt strangled by my timelines, details, and instructions. They were bright, mature professionals, and I was treating them like children. What they needed was for me to provide clear vision and boundaries, and then get out of the way.

When volunteers feel smothered or helpless, motivation and efficacy levels decrease. Volunteers may even decide that the benefits of volunteering no longer outweigh the amount of effort necessary for the role. As a result, they may quit or relocate to another opportunity where they do feel empowered. If you want to create a culture that retains volunteers, you will need to work hard at providing direction while simultaneously giving individuals the freedom to carry out the mission in the unique way God has created him or her. For the remainder of this chapter, let's talk about some ways to set volunteers free.

Describe a Defined Win

For a volunteer to be set free, he must know what success in his role looks like in specific and measureable terms. One way to do this is to write a win statement for each volunteer role. For parking attendants, this might be how many cars they should be able to fit in the lot. For a student small group leader, this could be establishing a number of contacts they should have with students during the week. Focus on taking your organization's big picture mission and vision, and providing specific answers to how this should be accomplished within each individual role.

Provide Clear Boundaries

Everyone moves with more confidence when boundaries are clearly marked and illuminated. Many of us are inclined to drive faster on a well-lit and marked freeway. Yet on a dark, country road, we move more slowly because our attention is absorbed searching for the edges, dangers, and potholes. When you let volunteers know their boundaries, you allow them to focus on their roles instead of searching for answers to questions like how much, how often, and for how long. The organization that has no

STRATEGY 4: EMPOWER THEIR PASSIONS

boundaries unknowingly removes freedom because the volunteer never knows what is acceptable, and will often defer to doing less rather than more.

Establish a Single Point of Accountability

Every volunteer needs to know to whom he or she is accountable. As leaders, we need to create clear and simple systems that provide volunteers with a clear understanding of who is their direct report. When a volunteer is accountable to several leaders, expectations are multiplied and can sometimes even lead to conflict.

In organizations where several leaders are present at the same time, it is important for each leader to understand who is on his or her volunteer team, and not overstep a place of authority. If there is an issue with a volunteer, the leader should address the volunteer's supervising leader and not the volunteer.

Have a Toolbox of Resources

All leaders of nonprofit organizations understand the tension between having what they need to function versus the amount of money in their budget. For this reason, the importance of providing volunteers with the tools necessary for their roles can sometimes get overlooked. These resources might look like books and articles to better equip your volunteers who are serving in relational roles. Or it might be a box or shed with real, physical tools.

Providing the tools necessary to complete the job communicates to volunteers you are expecting them to be successful and you value their time. Let's explore this idea through the example of a simple event like a spring cleanup day. The organization that is volunteer-minded will have stacks of rakes, wheelbarrows, and gloves ready to go. Every volunteer will be able to dive in and invest in a way that makes him feel like his contribution is valuable; as opposed to when there are not enough resources, and half of the group stands around feeling awkward for not working.

Sure, you may end up having a few extra rakes in the storage closet most days of the year, but you will outweigh the cost of those rakes by developing a culture that empowers teams to do massive projects. An empowered team of volunteers translates to massive savings for your organization's maintenance personnel and contract labor costs. In the world of volunteerism, it might cost money up front to save money in the long term.

Provide Feedback That Affirms

Providing affirming feedback goes a long way in helping a volunteer feel appreciated and supported, while reinforcing what is important to the leader. By praising the things that are important, leaders clarify the win and raise the bar. We have colleagues who model this so well. They walk through their areas and look for specific ways to cheer on and thank their volunteers. We hear them say things like:

- Thank you for dancing with your small group kids during song time. Seeing you engage in worship shows the kids that you love to worship Jesus too!
- Great job directing cars into those tricky parking spots in the left corner of the lot. That really makes traffic flow and helps people feel safe.
- Well done working sound. You really anticipate the audio cues and provide just the right punch. I feel confident on stage when I know someone like you is in the sound booth.

Keeping in mind that *what gets rewarded gets repeated,* consider how you can use public affirmation to shape your volunteer culture. For instance, I noticed a season when our kids ministry volunteers began to wear the team T-shirt inconsistently. When I asked why, the feedback I received varied from not liking to wear the same thing every week to disliking the color to just simply forgetting to bring it. One week I sent a special email, reminding everyone to please wear the team shirt that weekend. During Huddle, I made a huge deal out of the fact that they wore their shirts, and told stories I had heard the week before from families who were new to the church. For those families, the bright orange shirts helped them know where to bring their kids and who to ask for help. As a team, we agreed it was worth it to wear the team shirts, and the following week, everyone was back to sporting their loud, orange T-shirts.

Redirect When Necessary

It can feel awkward to tell a volunteer he is doing something incorrectly. After all, he is giving his time for free, to move forward the mission of your organization. However, failing to redirect incorrect actions can ultimately derail your mission. It is imperative that you provide clear and kind feedback that redirects and improves volunteer performance.

A key to providing redirection is for you as the leader to "own" the problem. In other words, you should approach issues that need redirection by considering your own responsibility in how things got off course. Often when a volunteer gets sideways on a project or task, it is because he has not been shown or given details as to how to carry out the task properly. So as you begin to redirect, consider opening with a phrase like, "*I am so sorry, I must have failed to show you . . .*"

When redirecting a volunteer, use a kind tone and be full of grace. Choose a time and place when there is opportunity for further conversation if necessary, and the volunteer will not feel embarrassed or reprimanded. Chances are he just needs a nudge back in the right direction. If for some reason, you feel like the volunteer is aware of his mistake and is intentionally choosing to act otherwise, check out our section on conflict resolution in Chapter 15.

Next Steps

1. What is something of which you are afraid to let go?

2. What resources in your ministry are missing, broken, or over complicated, keeping your volunteers from being able to fully succeed?

18 CUT THE RED TAPE

Fight to make volunteering an easy and enjoyable process by avoiding excessive forms, paperwork, permissions, and reports.

The Table

The previous chapter was about providing volunteers with clear direction, guidance, and boundaries in order to set them free to complete the mission of your organization. It should be our goal to make each individual's gifting and personality shine in his or her role. Now that we have established the boundaries necessary to know where we are going, let's talk about clearing the roadblocks that stand in our way.

Recently I (Darren) was leading an event at a church that had graciously allowed us to use its facility. The church had a small table display in the spot where we hoped to set up our store, registration, and help desks. I asked one of the staff members from the host church if it would be possible to move the table over to another location during the event, and I was floored to receive his response of, "That's way above my pay grade." Are you kidding me! I was dumbfounded. In fact, I had only asked if it was okay to move the table because I was being polite; I never dreamed I would be denied permission.

For the rest of the afternoon, I could not stop pondering the restrictive nature of a culture that requires forms and approvals to temporarily move a table. Maybe you are as flummoxed as me. But I bet within every organization, there is *the table*. Take a moment and ask yourself if there is anything your volunteer culture is holding too tight. Consider if you are allowing your volunteers freedom or saddling them with unnecessary forms, reports, meetings, policies, and permissions.

Removing Roadblocks

One of the primary responsibilities of a leader is to remove barriers and make it easy for volunteers to serve. Too often leaders give volunteers roles without the necessary resources and expect them to solve the deficiency. At times, we let things remain broken or under-resourced because we feel helpless. If you find yourself saying things like, "Oh yeah, that thing hasn't worked in months," or "that's not my department," then it's time to sharpen your scissors and start cutting the red tape.

At other times, we are actually the ones creating red tape because we desire control. I (Steph) can be a control freak. Sometimes I feel like I have it all figured out in my mind, and those who offer suggestions that require change are trying to make my head explode. But something I have learned from working with volunteer teams is that other people have brilliant ideas! It should not require several emails and conversations before I encourage a volunteer to try something new. My response to suggestions and ideas should be, *"That's a fun idea!"* and, *"Let's try it!"* far more often than it is, *"That's not gonna happen."*

Obviously, we don't think you should throw all of your policies, procedures, and values out the door every time a volunteer makes a suggestion or asks for a change. Part of being a leader is needing to sometimes say *no* in order to uphold the core values of your organization. What we are talking about here is cutting through the red tape. Red tape is defined as "excessive bureaucracy or adherence to rules and formalities." In other words, cutting the red tape means removing the obstacles that are impeding your volunteers from getting stuff done.

Great leaders remove existing roadblocks, and even greater leaders foresee obstacles and remove them before they become a hindrance. This week, take some time and walk through the areas in which your volunteers serve. Ask yourself the question, *"If I was a volunteer, what would I need removed or fixed in order to fulfill my role with excellence?"* Once you recognize a problem, become tenacious about solving it. Don't let budget, departmental permissions, or lousy excuses stand in the way of providing volunteers a clear path for performing their roles.

Asking for Feedback

Your volunteers are in the trenches, elbows deep in the nitty-gritty operations of your organization. Sometimes it can be easy to look from a distance and feel great about how your organization is running: attendance is up, social media is buzzing, and things are looking pretty stinkin' good. Before you get too comfortable, keep in mind that every organization has roadblocks of one kind or another. They might be small, but they are there; and if you want to know where roadblocks exist, just ask your volunteers!

Here are some questions you can use to invite feedback from your volunteers:

- What has surprised you most about being a volunteer?
- Do you have any general or specific observations about being a volunteer?

- Do you have the tools and resources necessary to perform your role?
- What do you enjoy the most about volunteering?
- What is your biggest frustration as a volunteer?

Once you have asked for feedback, be prepared to follow up. Solve as many problems and remove as many roadblocks as you can while remaining within the boundaries and parameters of your organization. Sometimes you will not be able to fulfill a request made by a volunteer, but make sure you have a conversation with that person to explain why it is not possible. When you ignore a request from a volunteer, she may feel like you don't value her opinion, drastically minimizing your chances of getting valuable feedback in the future.

Next Steps

1. Do your volunteers know to whom they report?
2. What roadblocks are you aware you need to remove?

19 MAKE IT HELPFUL

Focus on empowering volunteers to live well at work and home, and let weekend programming be an after-effect.

Get Your Volunteers Promoted

There is nothing more tedious than sitting through a meeting where the leader spends the entire time explaining how your team has been screwing up, and then outlines the step-by-step process that is going to fix it. Not only does it make the listeners feel like they are being treated as incompetent, but it usually doesn't solve the problem anyway.

When you plan your times with volunteers (which we sure hope you aren't calling trainings—see Chapter 8), use the opportunity to empower your volunteers and lift them up as individuals. A two-hour explanation on how to decipher curriculum or how to make a junky copier run cardstock isn't helpful for life. In fact, it simply reveals poor leadership and a lack of care for volunteers. The equipment you purchase and the processes you set in place should be volunteer-friendly and easy to use.

Training and input received during a volunteer experience should be beneficial beyond the specific volunteer role. Leaders should focus on empowering volunteers to live well at work and home, and let the volunteer experience be an aftereffect. The church and faith-based organizations should be places that equip for life. As you prepare for times of intentional investment into volunteers, ask yourself: **Will this training help them get a promotion at work?**

A recent study by the Corporation for National and Community Service explored the effect of volunteerism on job placement. They reported the following:

> In addition to improving the lives of neighbors and communities, volunteers can improve their own lives by gaining skills, experience, and contacts that can be helpful in finding employment. Our "Volunteering as a Pathway to Employment" study found that volunteers have 27 percent higher odds of finding a job after being out of work than non-volunteers. This effect may be due to developing new skills and expanding personal networks.

There are 168 hours in a week, and the average volunteer spends 2 of them helping you. The rest of the time they are employees, parents, caretakers, students, and countless other roles. As a leader, you should be providing value to their lives as a whole, not just the small slice they spend volunteering for your organization.

Going Beyond the Surface

There will be times you need to sit down with volunteers to review policies, provide training for a piece of equipment, or implement a system. However, keep in mind that your times together must still hold an inspirational and relational aspect. When providing direction, keep a tone of appreciation and confidence in volunteers. Avoid reprimanding the group or pointing out mistakes.

When it does become necessary to address issues that need to be corrected, think strategically. It is important you think about the

STRATEGY 4: EMPOWER THEIR PASSIONS

core issue as opposed to the symptom you are experiencing. The wise leader uses surface issues to guide them toward the true underlying problem. Ask yourself the hard questions first and focus on identifying the underlying values, assumptions, beliefs, and expectations that are producing the undesirable outcomes.

For instance, a difficulty in many organizations is volunteers arriving late. A common conclusion could be that volunteers aren't paying attention to the time or don't care about Huddle. However, reality might be that something outside of their control, like not having enough available parking, causes them to drive around outside your building looking for a spot. When you can solve the problem on your own, like adding more parking for volunteers, a training session isn't even necessary.

Another thing to note in resolving issues is to ask *who* is causing the problem. In order to avoid conflict, it can be tempting to use a training that speaks to all volunteers, rather than having a one-on-one conversation with a few. When we do this, the majority of volunteers feel discouraged and confused because they are being reprimanded for something they thought they did well.

Before addressing issues that are troubling you, take a moment and ask yourself *why* this is happening and *who* is causing the problem. Then do everything you can to resolve the issue for volunteers, rather than making it the problem of an entire team.

Where To Help

As you commit to developing your volunteers in ways that are helpful, think of areas where volunteer roles overlap with life at home and work. Here are five core areas in which we think most people engage, regardless of your organization's mission and your volunteers' stage in life.

Human Resources. Nearly every volunteer is responsible to provide leadership to someone else throughout the course of his or her work and professional life. Your investment in improving the volunteer's ability to listen, provide feedback, communicate, and empathize will be appreciated. Within her role, a volunteer should become adept at dealing with people different from her like kids, parents, or coworkers. She should be able to resolve issues quicker. She might even learn to listen more attentively and verbalize her feelings more appropriately.

Personality Types and Learning Styles. The more we understand the individual uniqueness of the people around us, the more equipped we are to build and maintain lasting and meaningful relationships. Exploring learning styles, personality types, and strength profiles are all ways to improve interaction both within volunteer and outside roles. You might consider introducing volunteers to profiles such as StrengthsFinder™, RightPath™, and the Myers-Briggs Type Indicator™. You will find the volunteer is appreciative of the investment in his life and success, and you will gain valuable insight into how to best empower him for ongoing success and retention.

Strategic Thinking. Your volunteers have dreams and goals. By introducing them to how your organization strategizes to meet its mission, you provide them vital information to not only be high-capacity supporters, but also to empower their dreams. Consider how you can share your strategy with volunteers by inviting them into the process through creative meetings and vision-casting events.

Conflict Resolution. We all want to learn how to better resolve pesky issues. Enlisting a counselor or mediator to teach volunteer teams conflict resolution techniques and approaches will reduce tension and improve performance. Not only will volunteers benefit from this in their roles at your organization, but principles can also be used to address relationships with friends, family, and coworkers.

STRATEGY 4: EMPOWER THEIR PASSIONS

Customer Service. Of all the places a person can visit, a faith-based nonprofit should be at the top of the list when it comes to customer service. Since your nonprofit has a vision bigger than dollars, it should be excellent at placing a priority on people's experiences. Since it is dependent on the partnership and generosity of others, it should ooze a spirit of friendliness. By the very nature of your mission, your organization is beautifully positioned to be a beacon of friendliness, grace, compassion, and acceptance. Teaching and modeling these principles will be of great benefit to your culture of volunteerism by providing a healthy atmosphere and giving volunteers the skills and attitudes necessary to excel in their workplaces.

Something important to note about the above five areas is that your organization is probably full of experts in those areas. We have found that educators are thrilled to share their experience because it assists them in their pursuits. Business executives are often looking for ways to share their knowledge in ways that provide eternal and community value. Your customer service experts are chomping at the bit to assist in training your teams because they want to invite their neighbors. Your artists are dying to suggest some makeover tips because, frankly, your choice of décor makes their skin crawl. You don't necessarily need to fly experts in from around the country. Simply access the professionals you already have in your presence and assist them in contextualizing the concepts to fit the specific needs of your volunteers' roles.

Next Steps

1. How is your organization positioned to provide knowledge and experiences that are helpful to volunteers in their roles at home and at work?

2. Who are professionals within your organization who could apply their expertise to situations your volunteers face?

THE VOLUNTEER PROJECT

20 VOLUNTEERS WHO MULTIPLY

Provide such an incredible volunteer experience that volunteers invite their friends to join them.

A Zero Recruitment Culture

Volunteers who multiply are those who feel significant, supported, and connected. They have found a place to pursue their passion of helping. This happens when leaders come alongside them and acknowledge their presence, praise their input, share stories of impact, and resource their ideas.

Our goal for *The Volunteer Project* is to help leaders create volunteer cultures in which they never have to recruit again. We want to help you stop recruiting and start retaining by creating an irresistible volunteer culture. The goal of leading volunteers should be to provide such an incredible volunteer experience that volunteers invite their friends to join them. We call that our **Zero Recruitment Model.**

Imagine what a zero recruitment culture would look like for you. Rather than sitting at your desk trying to think of who you can call to beg to fill a volunteer gap this weekend, you would have requests to serve popping up in your email inbox. Instead of combining volunteer teams, you would be equipping new leaders to resource the growing number of volunteers. The time you spend making pleas for new volunteers, you could now spend saying *thank you* to the ones who already exist.

A zero recruitment culture is dependent on volunteers feeling fully appreciated, supported, connected, and empowered. When volunteers are cared for, supported, and provided fun and meaningful experiences, they will invite their friends. People can't keep a good thing to themselves!

New Volunteer Process

In Chapter 6 we discussed the importance of having a process in place to integrate new volunteers into their roles. Once your Zero Recruitment Model is up and running, be sure you are ready for those newly invited volunteers to arrive! You want to make it easy for potential volunteers to begin the process at any time of day. There should be an online form, information packet, or action step that allows an interested person to take immediate action when he or she is ready.

Not only should it be easy for a potential volunteer to access information and contact you, all of your current volunteers should know exactly where to encourage friends to go to take action. When next steps are unclear, conversations often come to a halt with, "Oh, let me find out," because people either forget to follow up or change their mind while they wait for an answer.

Once a potential volunteer reaches out to you, be sure to respond expediently. Far too often we hear non-volunteers tell us about how they tried to volunteer but nobody responded, the process didn't make sense, or it seemed as though they were inconveniencing the person for whom they were attempting to volunteer.

STRATEGY 4: EMPOWER THEIR PASSIONS

Multiplication and Social Media

A recent American Express™ study reports that people will tell an average of fifteen people about a positive experience, and twenty-four people about a poor experience. This means your attempt to build a zero recruitment culture and multiply volunteers is dependent on your volunteers spreading the good word about your organization and its volunteerism experience.

We live in a world where people's best, and sometimes their worst, experiences are shared on social media. It doesn't take long for us to tell stories, share needs, and send invitations. I recently heard someone explain that if you have to spend money in advertising, you're doing something wrong. If you're doing the right stuff and taking care of people, people won't be able to stop talking about you! Positive word of mouth is worth its weight in gold. Chances are, your volunteers are already talking about you on social media. Here are some tips to help you capitalize on the chatter:

Provide easy-to-share content. If you want your volunteers to use social media to share stories and invite friends to join them, then you need to make social media a priority as well. Posting videos that share stories, give mid-week encouragement, and highlight your volunteers' investments can be powerful things to be shared and retweeted.

Have a hashtag. Combine the voices of everyone together by providing a unique hashtag for volunteers to use in their posts. Be sure to do research in advance to confirm your unique hashtag is not already being used. For instance, the hashtag #studentvolunteers will not gain you as much traction as #[nameofyourministry]studentvolunteers.

Ask people to share on a specific topic. If there is a certain aspect of your ministry that you would like everyone to be talking about, then go ahead and ask! Most people are willing to share about their volunteer experiences, but just don't think to do so on their own. Get people to point their friends toward volunteering by asking them to share on a topic. For instance, why they volunteer, the most unexpected thing that has ever happened as a volunteer, or why they show up each week.

Follow them. Okay, it does sound a little bit stalkerish, but how are you going to know what people are saying if you don't look? Great interaction with volunteers is built on relationships, and for many people, the digital world is a big part of their relationships. Take time each week to engage with volunteers online and interact with the stories they share.

Equipping Leaders

In the book of Ephesians, Paul writes about the leader's role in *equipping the saints*. He starts by reminding us of God's love and grace. The opening verses are full of incredible promises. Paul reminds us that it isn't by our own power or strength through which God's purposes are accomplished, but by God working through us. Our prayer for you is *that God will provide you with immeasurably more than you can ever dream or imagine*. Not only you, but also the volunteers you lead, are God's handiwork, created by Him to do good works. Our job is to create a framework in which His people can grow and thrive.

Next Steps

1. Can you connect a person to your new volunteer process with a Tweet?

2. Ask your volunteers what it would take for them to want to invite their friends to join them as volunteers.

IMAGINE IF...

Imagine with us a day when your organization is full of volunteers whose stories of life change are so contagious, you never have to awkwardly beg people to join. You're surrounded by a zero recruitment culture where volunteers have the support they need, feel empowered to perform their roles, have a strong sense of community, and are experiencing significance and meaning. There's an indescribable buzz in the hallway! There's a sense of anticipation! Your organization is a magnet for new, high-level volunteers, and you have created a system that develops leaders.

Sounds amazing, right? Yeah it does! So let's reshape our thoughts and actions so we are leading in a manner that benefits volunteers, guests, and our families. In fact, right now is a great time to take the first of many wonderful steps.

How would that impact the quality of . . . .
    your programming?
    your family life?
    your stress level?
    your feelings about the work you do?

Remember that the changes and improvements you make today will directly impact the vibe of your organization's culture tomorrow. As a leader, you are paving the way and setting the course for the future growth of your organization. How will you begin to **stop recruiting** and **start retaining?**

LOOKING FOR MORE?

We are thrilled to stay on this journey with you. Consider expanding your knowledge and experience through one, some, or all of the options below.

Read the dissertation that started it all. *The Volunteer Project* is inspired by Darren's doctoral dissertation on volunteer satisfaction. If you would like a full bibliography of volunteer documents, as well as research methodology, zip over to Amazon and grab *Impact of Best-Practices Management of Volunteers on Volunteer Satisfaction in a Church Setting (2012)* by Dr. Darren Kizer.

Schedule a consultation. Maybe statistics and data aren't your thing. Maybe you just want to talk to a real person. Let's schedule a time for one of our experts to visit you onsite to complete a site assessment and consultation.

Host a HuddleUP Volunteer Event. So you have identified some gaps, but feel like you could benefit from your team hearing from an outside voice. We would love to join you and your team onsite, to assist you in leading a HuddleUP event for your volunteers and leadership.

Take a class. Have you been thinking about earning a master's degree or are just an education junkie? Consider signing up for a college course in volunteerism through Orange Academics. Darren loves teaching these courses, utilizing a blend of distance education methodologies and hands-on experiences.

Discover more and connect with us at StopRecruiting.com.

RESOURCES AND REFERENCES

INTRODUCTION

- Adrian Swinscoe's customer and employee engagement consulting firm: www.adrianswinscoe.com/not-many-complaints-but-still-losing-customers/
- TARP Worldwide, 1999

CHAPTER 4

Spear, S. (2009). *The High-Velocity Edge.* New York: McGraw-Hill.

CHAPTER 5

- McCloud, C. (2006). *Have You Filled A Bucket Today?* Northville, MI: Ferne Press.
- Carnegie, D. (1981). *How To Win Friends and Influence People.* New York: Simon and Schuster. (A classic resource.)

CHAPTER 6

- Mark Brooks is a consultant with the Charis Group. www.thecharisgroup.org
- Wideman, J. *Children's Ministry Leadership.* Loveland, CO: Group Pub., 2003. Print. (Wideman's writings are full of practical wisdom and inspiration.)

CHAPTER 9

Crabtree, J. (2008). *Better safe than sued.* Grand Rapids, MI: Zondervan. (Jack has done a masterful job of making challenging legal principles easy to understand for staff and volunteers.)

CHAPTER 10

- Read Exodus 18 to learn more about Moses and Jethro.
- Ephesians, Paul's letter to the church in Ephesus, addresses the ideas of preparing and equipping.

CHAPTER 11

- Stuart Hall is a gifted speaker and writer: www.theechogroup.com
- Hybels, B. (2004). *The Volunteer Revolution.* Grand Rapids, MI: Zondervan.
- Searcy, N., & Henson, J. (2007). *Turning First-Time Guests Into Fully Engaged Members of Your Church.* Ventura, Calif.: Regal Books.

CHAPTER 12

- Joiner, R. (2013). *Playing For Keeps/Losing Your Marbles.* Cumming, GA: Orange.
- ReThink Group: www.thinkorange.com

CHAPTER 13

Clark, C. (2011). *Hurt 2.0.* Grand Rapids, MI: Baker Academic.

CHAPTER 15

- Cloud, H., & Townsend, J. (2003). *Boundaries face to face.* Grand Rapids, MI: Zondervan.
- Andy Stanley: *Trust vs. Suspicion* podcast https://itunes.apple.com/us/podcast/andy-stanley-leadership-podcast/id290055666 (A great resource on managing conflict.)
- Pilgrimage Educational Resources: www.simplyapilgrim.com

CHAPTER 19

- Spera, C.; Ghertner, R., Nerino, A., DiTommaso, A. (2013). Volunteering as a Pathway to Employment: Does Volunteering Increase Odds of Finding a Job for the Out of Work? Corporation for National and Community Service, Office of Research and Evaluation: Washington, DC, 2013
- Corporation for National and Community Service: www.nationalservice.gov/impact-our-nation/research-and-reports/volunteering-america
- Strengths Finder: Gallup Press. www.strengthsfinder.com
- Right Path Resources: www.rightpath.com
- MBTI: Meyers & Briggs Foundation, Gainesville, Florida. www.myersbriggs.org

CHAPTER 20

Findings from a recent American Express study: http://about.americanexpress.com/news/pr/2012/gcsb.aspx

We would also like to thank FISH, reThink Group, and Pilgrimage Educational Resources, for how their philosophies have shaped the way we view and interact with volunteers.

ABOUT THE AUTHORS

Darren Kizer, EdD

As Orange's Director of Strategic and Academic Initiatives, Darren's primary focus is on forming new partnerships and helping the leaders of unique ministry strategies win. Prior to joining the staff at Orange, Darren spent 10 years as the Executive Family Ministries Pastor of a growing multi-site church in Pennsylvania. He's passionate about volunteerism and education, and holds a doctorate focused on volunteerism, family ministry, and leadership. He and his wife, Becky, have two grown children, Brynn and Tucker. In his spare time, Darren can be found building something (the more tools the better), drag racing his VW Thing, or relaxing with friends at the lake.

Social: @darrenkizer

Christine Kreisher

Christine serves as the Executive Director of Ministries at GT Church, a thriving multi-site church in Reading, Pennsylvania. In her role, she provides strategic direction and visionary leadership, including family ministry and adult discipleship. Passionate about developing leaders to influence the next generation, her mission is to help people find and live God's unique purpose for their lives! Christine is a dynamic, authentic communicator who has been the featured speaker for numerous local, regional, and national conferences including The Orange Conference and SALT. Her diverse life and business experiences have allowed her to coach and connect with audiences around the world, ranging from church leaders and volunteer teams to corporate executives. Christine enjoys traveling and fishing with her best friend and business partner, Jim. They were flippin' houses before it was cool and have owned a coffee shop for the past 23 years all while raising three pretty awesome guys!

Twitter: @christinekreish
Instagram: @ckreisher

Steph Whitacre, M.A.

With over a decade of experience leading students and volunteers, Steph now spends her days investing in church leaders and families as part of the Orange team—primarily as the Content Editor for Orange Academics. Prior to joining Orange, she was on staff at Parker Hill Church as their Family Ministries Coordinator and Family Map Champion. Steph earned a bachelor's degree in counseling from Summit University, and went on to complete a master of arts. One of her favorite things is helping brilliant people zero in on ideas and share their stories. When she isn't reading, writing, or editing words, she can be found running, planning adventures with friends, and drinking coffee. Steph lives in metro Atlanta with her husband, Tim, and their son, Landon.

Blog: stephwhitacre.com
Social: @StephWhitacre